# 10 Wa,~~~~~~

# Broke ... Forever

# 10 Ways to Stay Broke . . . Forever

*Why Be Rich When You Can Have This Much Fun?*

**Laura J. McDonald and Susan L. Misner**

WILEY

Library and Archives Canada Cataloguing in Publication

McDonald, Laura, 1978-

    10 ways to stay broke—forever : why be rich when you can have this much fun? / Laura J. McDonald and Susan L. Misner.

Includes index.
Issued also in electronic formats.
ISBN 978-1-118-58653-2

    1. Finance, Personal.    2. Budgets, Personal.    I. Misner, Susan, 1971– II. Title.   III. Title: Ten ways to stay broke—forever.

HG179.M3248 2013           332.0240082           C2013-900797-0

ISBN 978–1–118–58658–7 (ebk); 978–1–118–58660–0 (ebk); 978–1–118–58661–7 (ebk)

**Production Credits**
Managing Editor: Alison Maclean
Executive Editor: Karen Milner
Production Editor: Pauline Ricablanca
Cover Design: Wendy Mount and Adrian So
Front cover image: Jar © Mark Viker/Getty Images; Pennies © Susan Findlay/Getty Images
Back cover image: Adrian So
Composition: Thomson Digital
Printer: Dickinson Press

Printed in the United States of America

1 2 3 4 5 DP 17 16 15 14 13

To our wonderful families, supportive husbands and "golden" readers who allow us to go for broke every day ... to give it our all, share our voice and build a community that inspires, impassions and propels our lives.

# Contents

# Preface

## A World of Debt Gone Wild

We're baaaaaaack! Only one year after the fantastic response to our first book, *It's Your Money, Honey: A Girl's Guide to Saving, Investing, and Building Wealth at Every Age and Life Stage*, we are back, and this time not just for the girls!

Our mission has always been to help more women take ownership of their finances and gain control of their financial destiny. This has not changed. Following the publication of *It's Your Money, Honey*, we were thrilled, gratified and uplifted by the huge outpouring of support from our readership, the financial community and the public at large. What surprised us the most was the volume of wonderful feedback we received from male readers. It seems they have been reading over your shoulders, ladies!

Well, gentlemen, forgive us if we have neglected you. We recognize that just because the financial industry has long been dominated by men, that certainly does not mean that *all* men have a grasp on their personal finances. As a result, we made sure that this time around, our book focuses not only on women, but on *everyone* who wants to gain more control over their financial destiny.

The rise in household debt across Canada is a serious issue that affects every woman, man, child and pet. Yes, even our furry friends suffer the consequences. (You know that look you get when you try to substitute a cheaper brand of kibble . . .) We wanted to tackle the issue of dealing with debt in a way that motivates *all* our readers to improve this critical area of their life.

Once we decided to focus our new book specifically on debt management, the question we faced was how to approach it. How could we take a potentially boring topic and make it fresh, relevant and motivating for our readers? Inspiration came from an article we published on our website, www.GoldenGirlFinance.com, in November 2011. It was called (you guessed it) "10 Ways to Stay Broke—Forever: Why Be Rich When You Can Have This Much Fun?" (Kudos to the brilliant gal behind this witty prose, Ms. Tara Struyk!)

The article received hundreds of thousands of views in just a couple days, tons of glowing comments and thoughtful emails from readers (male and female) expressing their appreciation for this clever take on a rather overhyped subject. We realized there would be no better way of approaching our second book and addressing the topic of debt management than to take one of our most popular articles and really run with it. Indeed, the response to our "10 Ways to Stay Broke" article is an ideal example of how we engage our readership in a fun and sometimes irreverent way. But there is always message to our madness! Under our charming and witty exterior (if we do say so ourselves), we deliver vital information and tips to those readers whom other financial media fail to reach.

The Task Force on Financial Literacy found that, overall, the commitment to financial education is uneven across the financial sector and its industries. And when financial education is provided, it tends to be technical, overly complex and written in obscure, jargon-filled prose. As a result, it often fails to reach the very people for whom it is designed.

This is where Golden Girl Finance comes in.

Golden Girl Finance is a platform to educate, inspire and motivate people into taking ownership of their finances, by putting a fresh, modern and feminine spin on financial literacy. As the voice of female finance for numerous national online, print and television platforms, as well as through our signature web property www.GoldenGirlFinance.com, the Golden Girl Finance brand reaches millions of readers, engaging and propelling them into financial action.

The same mission drives this book. We hope that by reading these words, you will be inspired to think and feel differently about your personal debt. For one thing, we want to take away the shame and stigma around talking about debt. Struggling with how to get your finances under control can be an incredibly stressful and lonely experience. We want to fling the doors open and shine a light on these dark and scary topics and show you how proper debt management, living within your means and accumulating cash rather than spending it are your keys to living a much richer life.

There has never been a better time to talk about debt. If you've ever thought you were alone in your struggle to pay the bills, you could not be more wrong. The personal debt load of Canadians is growing at a frightening rate. Household debt-to-income ratios have never been higher. And it's not just individuals—entire countries are struggling with unsustainable levels of debt. It seems we have become a society far too dependent on borrowing to solve our problems and fund our desires. We are living in a world of debt gone wild.

It is time to get back into balance—countries, households and individuals. This book will help you to examine the daily financial decisions you make that end up having a profound long-term impact on your financial stability and sense of security. Every day you make decisions that will either keep you in debt, put you further into debt or, ideally, get you out of debt and back on the path to building wealth. Most importantly, we approach these lessons on your terms. We start with the basics, help you to understand the key principles and show you how to build a healthy and solid foundation for your future.

Do you remember the Occupy Wall Street protests of 2011? Their participants wanted corporations and governments to take responsibility for the global financial crisis, the ensuing lack of accountability and the growing disparity between rich and poor. The Occupy protests became a global movement and an outlet for the frustrations of the "99 per cent" of the population around the world who were tired of government overspending and corporate greed taking a toll on their economy. *Our* economy. The Occupy movement was successful in voicing our collective desire for governments and corporations to get their act together and be more accountable, more far-sighted and more responsible in their financial decision-making.

But as our dear old granny used to say, what is good for the goose is also good for the gander. It is high time we all *personally* took a little more responsibility when it comes to our finances. Stop overspending and get those debt levels under control. Get our own act together! Occupy our chequing accounts!

And maybe, just maybe, together we can turn this economy around. One credit card statement at a time.

Laura and Susan

# Introduction

## Cash Flow Mojo

So. You have no savings or investments—and you haven't even thought about retirement! But hey, you have a new car, a beautiful new house and enough power suits to last you until you're 100 years old. Plus, you still have plenty of available credit. Who cares about the bottom line when life is this good?

It's a good question, and one that many people aren't forced to consider—until it's too late. Check out the top ways you can keep the charade going and stay broke! Yes, broke! If you're lucky, you'll die before anyone notices...

## 1. Finance Everything

Live for the now. If you can get a loan or buy something on credit, do it. This should be easy; after all, your salary isn't nearly big enough to cover all your "needs."

## 2. Pay the Minimum—on Everything

Take a look at your credit card statement. It should tell you how long it will take you to pay off the balance if you make the minimum payment. Shoot for a time frame that's longer than you can ever imagine living. That should do it. Now go have fun!

## 3. Spend It All

Financial advisers tend to recommend that you save up for things you want. That's impractical if you want things *right now*—now isn't it?

## 4. Buy a Huge House

Why have a smaller house when you can afford the mortgage payments on a bigger one by choosing the longest amortization possible? If you're lucky, the market will rise, giving you some extra equity to spend!

## 5. Buy a New Car

Car models don't change much year to year, but you can't put a price on that new-car smell. Ideally, you should be sporting a new ride every two or three years and financing it (of course!) for the longest term possible. If you do this for long enough, you may end up owing more than your car is even worth. That's okay—you'll look great doing it!

## 6. Take a Vacation

Pull out your credit card and go somewhere nice. There's nothing better than getting away from it all, and you totally deserve it! After all, you want to be able to brag about this for years to come. (Plus, you look great with a tan...)

### 7. Buy More Toys

A great car is important, but what you *really* want to shoot for is a motorhome pulling a truck, pulling a trailer with two ATVs inside (and possibly a boat, too). Then you'll know you've arrived—and you can arrive on any terrain you want!

### 8. Pay More When You Can

Rather than worrying about saving a dollar here and there, just do what is most convenient. Coupons, shopping around and waiting for things to go on sale is such a pain—and why bother for only a few dollars? After all, time is money!

### 9. Shop Every Day

Treat yourself whenever you get the chance. After all, nothing feels better than coming home with something new at the end of a hard day. If you can't find a use for what you've bought, you can always add it to your gift closet. You do have a gift closet, right?

### 10. Eat Out

Treat yourself to dinner out at least a few times a week. It's convenient, it's relaxing and your time is worth something—even if you wouldn't have spent it working.

### You Earned It?

That feeling of being on top is something only money can buy. Don't miss out. Money is made to be spent. After all, you earned it...right?

Reality check.

Okay, *wrong!* This is where common sense (finally!) kicks in. If there's anything that feels amazing, it's knowing you have money in the bank. The ultimate luxury is not a new car, designer wardrobe or scarlet-soled shoes; it's savings pure and simple. Don't you know that excessive spending went out of style with shoulder pads, teased bangs and "Dynasty"?

## Here's Looking at You, Kid

What you just read? That was the venerated article we spoke about . . . the namesake of this book and the one that ignited a flame in the broke(n) hearts and bank accounts of our readers.

Now, we are not here to judge (well, maybe the teased bangs). We know you work hard. You spend a huge portion of your life caring for other people. You rarely do anything for yourself. So when it comes to splurging on the latest iPad or splashing out on a five-star hotel for the holidays, *of course you deserve it!* There is no question. Buying new things makes you feel great . . . for awhile anyway. And then two things happen: the novelty wears off and you need another fix. And, if you bought the item on credit, you don't feel great when you have to pay off the balance—especially if you lack the cash to pay it off in full and must pay interest. If you go into debt over a purchase, you will never feel quite as amazing as you would if you could afford the item outright.

Buying something you don't have the cash for means you can't afford it. You know this intellectually, but sometimes we like to rationalize things in our head and fool ourselves into thinking we can afford them. We confuse having room on the credit card with affordability. But deep inside, you know the difference. It starts out as a niggling twinge of guilt. It grows to the kind of back-of-your-head stress that you might be able to control by day. By the middle of the night, however, it wakes you up and refuses to let you sleep. The bigger the debt, the bigger the stress. How will you pay for it? What will you not be able to pay for as a result?

The guilt. The remorse. The regret.

Every time you put down that piece of plastic, you might want to think about whether or not purchasing the item and adding to your debt will cause you regret later. Then think of Humphrey Bogart at the end of *Casablanca:* "Maybe not today, maybe not tomorrow, but soon and for the rest of your life."

Okay, maybe that's a bit dramatic, but if you've ever loaded yourself up with debt and struggled without the cash to cover it, then you know how boarding a plane to Lisbon in the middle of the night might seem like not such a bad idea.

## It's Not Just You

Speaking of Lisbon...if you've read a newspaper over the last few years you probably have heard about Europe being on the brink of disaster. Each month nervous investors (and some relatives!) watch to see which European country might go bankrupt or cause the euro to collapse.

While the European debt crisis may seem like something far away and complicated, at the heart of it, it's very simple. These countries did not bring in enough income, through taxes or other sources, to pay for their programs and the business of running their governments. They spent more than they earned. So they did what a lot of people do when they are short of cash: they borrowed. They issued bonds to investors, promising to pay back the money with interest. When that wasn't enough, they borrowed from other governments and banks. The more they borrowed, the more interest they had to promise in order to convince someone to lend them more money.

After awhile, these countries owed so much that they couldn't even afford to pay the debt servicing costs—otherwise known as interest payments. What happens then? Two choices: either a country gives up and goes into bankruptcy, or an organization, such as the International Monetary Fund (IMF), agrees to bail them out on the condition that the country goes on an austerity program—cutting way back on their spending. The equivalent of cutting up their credit cards.

So you see, if the entire country of Greece can go on an austerity program, so can little old you. Better yet, you can start your program *before* you find yourself teetering on the edge of bankruptcy.

## The Ultimate Luxury

But we do like nice things, don't we?

Imagine for a moment that you could have the most powerful and lasting luxury good on earth. Something that would make your life stress-free, boost your self-confidence and even make you irresistible to the opposite sex. You must have it, right? Are you pulling out your credit card right now? Stop right there! This luxury is the antithesis of credit card spending. It is called surplus cash flow and it is the ultimate luxury.

We're not kidding. Spending less than you earn can actually make you happier, healthier and feeling groovier than a weekly deep tissue massage at the best spa in town. Knowing you have money in the bank puts a spring in your step. It relaxes you and increases your personal magnetism. It gives you the *mojo*.

Skeptical? Think about someone—yourself or someone you know—who struggles with cash flow anxiety. You know the symptoms: nervous, awkward and constantly tallying up numbers mentally, while praying the credit card transaction will go through. Not cool. Not calm. Not confident.

Cash flow anxiety comes when your mind is constantly preoccupied with making it through to the next paycheque. It causes bags under your eyes from sleepless nights wondering how you can shift your credit card and overdraft balances between one another. And it causes you to lose your grip on reality when, despite your absolute lack of cash, you still find yourself seriously fretting about upgrading to the new iPhone or leasing a nicer car.

If you think the mental gymnastics required for this kind of rationalizing and creative financing don't take a toll on your physical and emotional health, you're fooling yourself. Think of it as a bad date. If you wake up in the morning and feel empty, it just wasn't worth it. We think you deserve better. You deserve to have the peace and energy that comes from living an honest and free life, unconstrained by the perils of debt.

You need to turn your cash flow anxiety into cash flow mojo.

## Time Is a Luxury, Why Not Cash?

Of course you've heard that time is money. More is always better, right? Having a surplus of time has a very similar effect on a person as a surplus of money. It's healthier and keeps you out of desperate situations.

Think for a moment what it feels like when you have a shortage of time. You are running late for an appointment. You rush around, can't find your keys, forget your phone. You drive like a maniac to your meeting, worrying about being late and freaking out over traffic or road construction. You pull into the closest parking lot and get into a fight with the machine that spits out your credit card. When you finally arrive at your appointment, you apologize profusely when the meeting starts and again when it ends. And you spend the rest of the day feeling like a general loser.

Now think about what it's like when you have extra time. Ahhh... is that the sound of birds singing? You've calmly gathered everything you need before heading out the door. You might leave early enough to walk to your appointment, getting a little burst of those happy-feeling endorphins, and giving you time to think about what you want to say and accomplish in your meeting. You arrive with a few blessed extra minutes to pick up a coffee, check your texts and respond to any urgent emails. You are calm, in control and a pleasure to be around.

As you can see, time *is* a luxury. It can have a huge effect on the way you feel about yourself and the way you present yourself to the world. The cash flow mojo works the same way. With surplus cash you can be free from being a slave to interest payments and the need to allocate your disposable income toward previous expenditures. (Who wants to pay for yesterday's stuff? So boring.) You can liberate that precious headspace for more noble pursuits (homemade nachos, anyone?).

Surplus cash gives you the liberty to buy gifts and treats for yourself outright and pay for vacations in advance, so they can be truly enjoyed without the stress of looming bills hanging over every pina colada.

Surplus cash means you can use your credit card the way heaven intended you to use it. Pay your bills on the card, earn points or cashback bonuses and use your cash to pay off the balance *in full* each month, avoiding interest charges entirely.

Most importantly, surplus cash becomes the foundation upon which you build your long-term financial security. By investing it in a long-term savings plan you will allow your savings to grow, thanks to the beauty of compound interest. Don't be surprised to feel your own confidence grow right along with it.

Having regular surplus cash will lead you to true financial independence—increasing your ability to have the experiences you always dreamed of: taking time off work, changing careers, becoming a philanthropist or travelling the world.

You deserve this.

Have we convinced you yet? If yes, then you are probably wondering exactly how you are going to attain this remarkable luxury of surplus cash. Fortunately for you, we are only at the beginning of this book. However, just to give you a glimpse into what's coming up, we will tell you this much: there are really only two ways to get more cash—by earning more and spending less.

Ouch, right?

Don't worry, honey. We are going to focus on spending smart and increasing your knowledge so that you can become more intuitive about making decisions that keep you out of debt and help you to create more surplus cash in your life.

Sound good? Let's get started…

# 1

## Finance Everything

*Live for the now. If you can get a loan or buy something on credit, do it. This should be easy; after all, your salary isn't nearly big enough to cover all your "needs."*

In 2007, just prior to the financial crisis that set off a global recession from which the world has still not fully recovered, an innovative web-based loan broker called Lending Tree released a television advertisement. It featured a smiling, clean-cut, white, middle-aged man enjoying an affluent-looking life in the burbs. He said something like this: "I'm Stanley Johnson. I've got a great family. I've got a four-bedroom house in a great community. Like my car? It's new. I even belong to the local golf club. How do I do it?" As he skims his backyard swimming pool, Stanley cheerfully says, "I'm in debt up to my eyeballs." While he calmly barbecues a meal for his wife and three children, he leans into the camera and says, "I can barely pay my finance charges." Finally, he rides off on his lawn tractor and through his perma-grin, pleads: "Somebody help me."[1]

We don't know where Stanley is now, but we are here to help you! Let's start with an explanation of the various types of financing that exist.

## More than Just Credit Cards

There are so many ways to get into debt! Many people unwisely use their high-interest credit card for all their financing needs, but there is a whole range of credit options, some of which might be more appropriate for your situation. Let's examine them.

### 1. Term Financing

This a loan provided by a bank or financial institution that requires you to pay back the funds on a specific payment schedule. The interest rate is not typically fixed and is subject to change along with the bank's lending rates. Term loans are typically structured for one to 10 years at most. Term financing is useful for small businesses that need help getting up and running. *Use only when necessary.*

### 2. Personal Line of Credit (PLC)

The good thing about PLCs is that, like credit cards and unlike loans, they only put you into debt if you use them: you can keep a PLC hanging around for years. Just don't confuse having access to cash with actually having cash. If you draw on your PLC you will owe interest. Usually the interest rate will be lower than the rate on

---

[1] www.LendingTree.com, "I'm in Debt Up to My Eyeballs," *YouTube* video, uploaded February 1, 2011, http://www.youtube.com/watch?v=r0HX4a5P8eE.

your credit card (think, 15–20 per cent lower!), making it a better choice for making a big purchase that you need to pay off over time. If you can't seem to shake off your credit card debt—shift your balance! Use your lower-interest PLC to pay off the higher interest card in full, then pay off the PLC as soon as you can. *Use strategically.*

### 3. Home Equity Line of Credit (HELOC)

This is one of those slightly worrisome forms of financing that often gets overused and is much abused. Basically, it is a way of creating a line of credit using the equity you've accumulated in your house. Interest rates on HELOCs are typically 0.5–1.0 per cent above the prime interest rate. Many people use a HELOC as a way to consolidate all their outstanding debt—including credit card debt, car loans and other personal loans—into one package. Other people use it to fund major purchases, such as home renovations or vacations.

While it is called a line of credit, a HELOC is really a second mortgage in disguise. Your home is your collateral and either your original mortgage will be amended to reflect the new debt or a second mortgage will be placed on your home. You cannot sell your home until you've paid back the HELOC debt in full. *Use cautiously.*

---

 **BEWARE OF EASY MONEY**

Because interest rates have been so low for the past several years, the easy access to cash through a HELOC has been irresistible to many homeowners. According to a 2011 poll, more than one-third

*(continued)*

of Canadian homeowners have set up a HELOC.[2] Yet a 2012 survey revealed that 29 per cent of those polled would have trouble making their mortgage and debt payments if interest rates were to rise by two points. If rates rose by three or four points, 58 per cent would be in trouble.[3] Furthermore, if house prices decline,[4] home equity will plummet too, potentially leaving heavily mortgaged homeowners in a perilous "negative equity" situation ... meaning the amount they owe on their home could potentially be more than their home's selling price. Yikes! Remember that little ol' housing crisis in the United States? Negative equity was a major contributing factor to the meltdown.

## 4. Peer-to-Peer Lending

This is the new kid on the block when it comes to debt financing. Also known as P2P lending (how hip and cool is that?), financial services websites such as www.IOUCentral.com connect investors with borrowers for both short- and long-term financing. Typically, P2P lending is used by small businesses looking for investors, but hey, your case to seek funding to buy a modest, one-bedroom villa in the Bahamas might have real merit! *Use for business.*

---

[2] Lisa Mills, "Canadians Lack Knowledge about Home Equity Lines of Credit," *Canada News Wire* (website), November 15, 2011, http://www.newswire.ca/en/story/877853/canadians-lack-knowledge-about-home-equity-lines-of-credit-but-only-one-in-ten-seek-expert-legal-advice-poll-reveals.

[3] Alexandra Posadzki, "Canada Household Debt: Higher Interest Rates Would Be Problem for Nearly Half, Survey Says," The Canadian Press, July 17, 2012, http://www.huffingtonpost.ca/2012/07/17/household-debt-canada-interest-rates_n_1679724.html?utm_hp_ref=canada-business.

[4] Michael Babad, "Toronto, Vancouver House Prices to Sink 15% Over 23 years, TD Warns," *The Globe and Mail*, June 11, 2012, http://www.theglobeandmail.com/report-on-business/top-business-stories/toronto-vancouver-house-prices-to-sink-15-over-2-3-years-td-warns/article4246895.

## 5. Credit Cards

Oh, come on—you know this one! A little too well, perhaps? Credit cards are awesome when you use them correctly. By "correctly," of course, we mean using them to pay bills and purchase items, collecting your points and then paying off your balance with cash before the monthly due date. This way, you get all the benefits and pay none of the interest. We would also like to point out one little-known fact when it comes to credit cards. If you're willing to forego the perks and benefits, most banks will switch your card to a lower interest-rate version if you simply call and ask. They don't usually advertise these cards, but they exist. Oh yes, they do! Not that you need a lower interest rate, because you pay off your credit card balance in full every month before the due date, isn't that right? *Use only as advised.*

## 6. Payday Loans

What do you mean you don't have an emergency fund? If your basement floods or a car tire blows out and you don't have cash to take care of it, you might turn to a payday loan provider to borrow some quick funds. The provider will take a look at your last paycheque to determine how much they are willing to loan you—usually not more than $1,000, and never more than they think you can afford to pay back on your next payday, when it will be automatically debited from your chequing account. Along with a hefty surcharge for the privilege of using their services, of course: anywhere from $17–$25 per $100 borrowed. *Proceed with extreme caution (or not at all). Can turn into a very bad habit!*

## Rainy Days

Cash flow mojo comes from having the security and confidence of knowing you have access to cash when you need it. Your own stash of cash—it's not borrowed. You never need security and confidence more than when faced with a crisis. Yet 92 per cent of Canadians say they would need to rely on some form of debt to raise $2,000 for an emergency.[5] Apparently using credit has become more popular than saving for a rainy day. No wonder everyone needs those posters reminding them to stay calm!

---

**⚷ GOLDEN RULE: EMERGENCY FUND**

Thou must have an emergency fund. You need enough money to cover at least three months of living expenses—six would be better. Stash the cash in a high-interest savings account with its own separate debit card and keep the card in a safe spot away from your wallet. This way, you won't be tempted to use the money for non-emergencies (cashmere sweater sales at Holt Renfrew are *not* technically emergencies). See "Liquidity Ratio," below.

---

## The Financial Fitness Assessment

Anyone who has ever joined a gym has likely gone through that horrible hazing ritual, euphemistically called "the fitness assessment." You know what we're talking about. The one where a super-buff 20-year-old watches while you jog on a treadmill, weakly attempt a chin-up and prove how many push-ups you can't do, before they bring out a medieval-looking set of calipers to pinch the fat under your arm. *Shudder.*

Rest assured, we would never subject you to such indignities. We have our own instruments of torture. Because if there is one point on which we agree with the gym rat, it is that in order to measure

---

[5] Douglas Hoyes, "Debt: The New Normal," *The Money Finder* (blog), September 24, 2012, http://themoneyfinder.ca/debt-the-new-normal-infographic.

your progress, we need to know where you are starting from. These five financial ratios will shine a light on what is really going on with your financial situation. Are you overspending, and if so, where? We need to locate exactly where the imbalance is taking place in order to help you find your balance.

## 1. Net Worth

**Goal: Positive (or at least trending positive).** Think of this as a temperature reading of your financial health. Regardless of how much you earn (or don't), how much you owe (or don't), and how good things might appear on the surface (big home with a shiny new car in the driveway), the calculation of your net worth cuts right through the mystery and lays bare the truth about how financially sound you are.

The calculation is very simple:

$$\text{assets (what you own)} - \text{liabilities (what you owe)} = \text{net worth}$$

Just to make sure you don't forget anything, these are the three categories of assets:

- **Liquid assets.** This always makes us think of the bottle of Patrón Gold tequila stashed in our freezer, but that's not really relevant here. Liquid assets means anything that is already cash or could be easily turned into cash. This includes money in your chequing and savings accounts and the value of all your investments, including stocks, bonds, mutual funds, exchange-traded funds (ETFs) or guaranteed income certificates (GICs) that you hold in trading accounts or tax-free savings accounts (TFSAs).

- **Long-term assets.** This includes the investments that are blocked off for you to use at some future date and that you cannot easily convert into cash. For example, investments within a registered retirement savings plan (RRSP), registered education savings plan (RESP), registered retirement income fund (RRIF), a life insurance policy or a pension plan.

- **Hard assets.** No, your enviable butt does not count, though it certainly ought to be worth something! We're talking about your bottom *line* here. These are tangible things you have accumulated that contribute to your wealth. Examples include your home, vehicles, jewellery, artwork, electronics, appliances, furnishings, vintage wines and anything else you could conceivably sell for a pretty penny. The caveat here, however, is that you may only include the value of items you *own* and not those you lease or rent.

Now for the uncomfortable part: your liabilities. Make a list of everything you owe money on: the mortgage on your home or cottage, those things you lease or rent, student loans, credit card debt, personal loans, lines of credit, department store cards, unpaid taxes and the money you still owe your dear old dad for the loan he gave you last year.

Once you've totalled everything up, simply take the value of your assets and subtract the value of your liabilities. Do you get a negative number or a positive number? Ideally, you want this number to be positive.

Don't panic if your net worth is negative. Many people who have recently bought a house and are in the early stages of paying off a giant mortgage have a negative net worth. Your goal is to gradually move this number into positive territory. Keep making those payments and check your net worth again in six months' time, or annually. Think of it as your weigh-in moment at Weight Watchers.

*Checklist: Ways to Improve Your Net Worth*

✓ Buy instead of rent. Increasing market value will give your assets a boost. Buyer beware, however: decreasing market value will lower the value of your assets.

✓ Pay down your mortgage faster and lower your liabilities.

✓ Eliminate credit card debt from your life and reduce your liabilities.

✓ Pay off your car loan as fast as possible in order to reduce the value of your loan (liability) faster than the value of the car (asset) depreciates.

✓ Put your money into savings and investments and let the powerful effects of compound interest grow your principal and increase the value of your assets.

✓ Take the free money! Many employers offer RRSP contribution-matching plans. Opt in and up your assets in the easiest, most painless way possible.

## 2. Debt-to-Income Ratio (A.K.A. Total Debt Service Ratio, A.K.A. TDS)

**Goal: Less than 40 per cent.** So let's go back to that liabilities column (oh, come on!). We all have some form of debt. Your debt-to-income ratio reveals whether or not your debt is at a healthy, manageable level for you. Put simply, this formula compares how much money you've got *coming in* with how much you've got *going out* every month.

From the list of liabilities in your net worth calculation, write down how much each of these debts costs you on a monthly basis. For example, your monthly credit card balance, the amount you pay on your mortgage or rent each month and your annual tax bill divided by twelve. Now add up your gross monthly household income. Start with your gross monthly salary (before deductions) and add your spouse's gross monthly salary. Add any other monthly income you regularly receive. This is your total gross monthly income. (Hopefully it's not too gross.)

Now divide your debt total by your income total and multiply by 100 to get a percentage:

(monthly debt payments ÷ monthly income) × 100

Got it? The lower the number, the better off you are. The bank considers a debt-to-income ratio (or total debt service ratio, as they sometimes call it) of 40 per cent or higher to be a sign of trouble. At that level, you are carrying more debt than is realistically sustainable given your income. Life starts to get very stressful. If anything happens to reduce your income, you could find yourself in a very awkward situation with your creditors.

Given that 40 per cent is the high-water mark for debt-to-income ratios, it might shock and appall you to learn that the average Canadian household's debt-to-income ratio is a whopping 163 per cent.[6] Seriously. So, yeah, this is a problem.

---

 **GOVERNMENT DEBT GONE WILD**

Think you've got debt stress? Try being the government of the United States. Through taxes and investments, the country generates *a lot*

*(continued)*

---

[6] Statistics Canada, "National Balance Sheet Accounts, Second Quarter 2012," *Statistics Canada* (website), n.d., http://www.statcan.gc.ca/daily-quotidien/121015/dq121015a-eng.htm.

of income: we're talking $2.17 trillion in 2011.[7] Yet in 2011, the U.S. government spent $3.8 trillion. Just look at all those zeroes:

U.S. tax revenue: $2,170,000,000,000

Federal budget: $3,820,000,000,000

New debt: $1,650,000,000,000

National debt: $14,271,000,000,000

Budget cuts: $38,500,000,000

Numbers like that are mind-boggling. So let's bring this down to our terms, shall we? If we remove a bunch of those zeroes, here is what this budget would look like in your household:

Annual family income: $21,700

Money the family spent: $38,200

New debt on the credit card: $16,500

Outstanding debt: $142,710

Family budget cutbacks: $385

It's a disaster, right? No family could survive for long on this budget without going bankrupt—and neither can a country. Now you can see why so many governments around the world are struggling with colossal debt crises. They need to earn more, spend less or both.

With government leaders acting so irresponsibly, is it any wonder that citizens aren't inspired to live within their own means? We as individuals must lead the way. We begin with getting our own houses in order. When we set the standard of financial stability for ourselves, we will expect the same standard from the officials we elect. Perhaps Mr. President might appreciate a copy of this book, hmmm?

---

[7] Tax Policy Center, Urban Institute and Brookings Institution, "Tax Facts: Historical Federal Receipt and Outlay Summary," April 13, 2012, http://www.taxpolicycenter.org/taxfacts/displayafact.cfm?Docid=200.

### 3. Housing Expense Ratio (A.K.A. Gross Debt Service Ratio or GDS)

**Goal: less than 32 per cent.** Are you familiar with the term "house poor"? You're house poor when too much of your disposable income goes toward your housing costs, leaving you with very little money at the end of the month for savings or other expenses. The term can apply not just to homeowners but to renters as well. Fortunately, this handy little expense ratio will measure how much you can reasonably afford to spend on housing.

Start with your gross monthly household income. This is the sum you arrived at previously when you calculated your debt-to-income ratio. Take your monthly mortgage payments (if you own) or your monthly rent (if you rent). Add to that any other regular monthly expenses associated with your home, such as utilities, taxes, insurance, condo and maintenance fees. Now, divide your monthly housing costs by your gross monthly household income and multiply by 100 to get a percentage:

$$(\text{Monthly housing costs} \div \text{monthly income}) \times 100$$
$$= \text{housing expense ratio}$$

The lower your percentage, the more affordable your housing situation is for you. The general rule of thumb is that anything that causes you to spend more than 32 per cent of your household income is *not affordable* and is putting you under a financial strain.

Take note that sometimes banks and financial advisers will call this ratio the "gross debt service ratio"—or "GDS," because they do love their acronyms. When you are considering buying a home or renting a new apartment, they will often reverse this ratio by taking your gross monthly household income and multiplying it by 0.32 in order to give you a maximum figure of what you can afford:

$$\text{gross monthly income} \times 0.32 = \text{maximum amount to spend}$$
$$\text{on all housing costs}$$

This will give you a guideline of what house price or rent you can consider when hunting for a new place to live.

## 4. Savings Rate

**Goal: 10 per cent or more.** For years, Canadian banks and financial advisers have drummed it into people's heads that they should be saving at least 10 per cent of their income every month. That's 10 per cent gross income at the very least—10 per cent of net income for the gold star. Unfortunately, for just as many years, Canada's average personal savings rate has been well below 5 per cent of annual income.

Now let's talk about you. Yes, you. To calculate your savings rate, take the amount of money you put into savings during one month and divide it by your monthly income. Multiply by 100 to get the percentage:

$$(\text{savings per month} \div \text{monthly income}) \times 100$$

In this equation, a bigger number is better. We don't want to put anyone on the spot here, but if your savings per month is zero and you'd like to know how much you *should* be putting aside in savings (as a minimum), just reverse the equation:

$$\text{monthly income} \times 0.10 = \text{minimum dollars to save each month}$$

If you've decided to be a real keener and save more than 10 per cent (we're so proud!), just multiply your monthly income by the percentage you want to save and you'll get your magic dollar figure.

---

**⚷ GOLDEN RULE: AUTOMATIC WITHDRAWALS**

Putting money aside into a savings account is never easy. There is always something more urgent, more demanding or more

*(continued)*

---

immediately gratifying that gets in the way of our best intentions. But imagine for a moment what you would do if you found out that your employer had implemented a mandatory savings plan, by which 5 or 10 or even 20 per cent of your paycheque would be automatically deducted and placed into a savings account for you. Before you say "I quit," remember, this is how you build wealth. You would make sacrifices. You would get by. You would figure it out. Best of all, you wouldn't have the stress and guilt of not adhering to your savings plan anymore: *it would just be taken care of.* Now go to your nearest bank and request a savings account with automatic withdrawals to coincide with your paydays. Go on, get!

## 5. Liquidity Ratio

**Goal: 6 or higher.** Last one, we promise—and then you can put away the calculator for awhile.

Remember the liquid assets you added up in your net worth calculation? (You're still thinking about the tequila in the freezer, aren't you? So are we!) A high level of liquid assets is an indication of healthy cash flow and, depending on your other long-term assets, potentially a strong financial situation. Basically, your liquidity ratio will tell you how long you could live off what you've presently got in cash, if life came to that. Which it won't. But the point here is to give you that feeling of cash flow mojo, baby.

Liquid assets are the ones you turn to in good times (a weekend getaway, a baby on the way, a down payment) and bad times (furnace conks out, car battery dies, bailing your high school buddy out of jail). Come to think of it, liquid assets *are* a lot like tequila, hmmm.

To calculate your liquidity ratio, start with the value of your liquid assets and divide by your monthly debt payments. (You previously added up your monthly debt payments when calculating your debt-to-income ratio.)

value of all your liquid assets ÷ monthly expenses = liquidity ratio

Ideally, your liquidity ratio will be six or higher. This means you have six months' worth of expenses on cash standby at all times. At least half of this should be placed into a dedicated emergency fund. Maybe throw a bottle of tequila in there too, just in case.

## So Now What? The Rehabilitation Plan

Okay, so you faced your fears, bit the bullet, gritted your teeth and did the calculations. Good for you! We commend you for your bravery. As they say in the 12-step programs, the first step is admitting.

So now what? What if you came out with a negative net worth, a debt-to-income ratio above 40 per cent, a housing expense ratio of more than 32 per cent and savings and liquidity ratios of zero? As we warned you in the Introduction, you really only have two strategies: earn more and spend less. How you choose to implement these two strategies is a matter to be determined by your own preferences and circumstances. You may want to enlist a professional financial planner to help you come up with tactics that work for your specific situation.

But hey, we're not going to leave you hanging! Here are a few thoughts on ways to earn more and spend less that might help to kick you into brainstorming gear. Remember, constraints just mean we have to be more creative.

### Earn More

Okay, so the first part of the equation is earning more. Easier said than done? That's up to you! Here are some tips to increase your worth:

- **Ask for a raise.** Make a business case to your boss to explain why your salary ought to be increased or request a performance-related bonus that you will work toward.

- **Find a new job.** Radical, yes, but sometimes checking job websites and meeting new people in your industry can uncover an opportunity for a higher-paying role that you didn't even imagine existed.

- **Moonlight.** More people than you realize take on extra jobs to get them through a tough financial spot. Maybe it's answering phones at the gym on the weekend or helping out at your sister-in-law's store in the evening. A regular supplement to income can make a big difference.

- **Create.** There's no reason to give away your talent when you can charge for it. Thanks to the online selling community, there is a 24/7 market out there of buyers. Build bookshelves, knit baby blankets, make jam. Make anything, make it well and get out there and sell it.

- **Teach.** Find a paying gig where you can share the expertise you've acquired. Teach classes at your community centre or offer online instruction. Whether it's how to make great cocktails or how to fix a car engine, focus on what you know best and can share with the world.

- **Sell your stuff.** As above, if you want to get all karmic about it, create more space in your life for the goodness to flow by clearing out old furniture and clothing. Be ruthless—do you really need that car or could you make do without it?

- **Learn a trade.** Further to the moonlighting concept, get some training and credentials to amp up your earning power and you might just end up launching a small business. Examples include yoga instruction, nutrition counselling, landscaping, catering, jewellery-making and bookkeeping. Sorry, guys, golfing probably isn't one of them.

## Spend Less

And now comes the second part of the equation . . . spending less. Here's how to create some savings:

- **Lower your interest rates.** This is one of those areas in life where those who ask, get. Interest rates are rarely carved in stone: there are always other accounts, other credit cards, other forms of loans and other financial institutions that you can choose from to get a better rate. Start by calling up your current financial institution and asking if they can do a little better on that interest rate for you. Ask them what your options are in terms of lowering your rate. Maybe you need to switch to a different form of financing. Find out what their competitors are offering. Often you can get a better rate just by moving more of your liquid or long-term assets into the same financial institution.

- **Pay less, more often, on your mortgage.** While this may feel like you are spending more, by paying off your mortgage as quickly as possible, you will end up wasting less money on interest. One way to do this is to shift your payment schedule from monthly to biweekly, adding a couple extra payments per year.

- **Never pay interest on your credit card.** Never carry a balance. Always pay off your monthly balance with cash. If you don't have the cash to buy an item, then you can't afford it. Put it back. If for some reason you must carry a balance, use a line of credit or other lower-interest form of credit to pay off the higher-interest credit card.

- **Evaluate your taxes.** Have you ever thought to yourself, something's missing? Deductions, we mean. So many of your financial decisions have tax implications and you would be wise to pay a little money to a tax adviser who can show you the way to a big, fat refund. Or, you could just give more of your money to the government. Whatevs.

- **Consider consolidation.** If your debt-to-income is seriously straining you, it might be time for a debt consolidation, putting everything into one easy-to-pay loan. The lower interest rate will mean you can pay down your principal faster and waste less money on interest, getting you to your debt-free goal faster.

- **Invest for income.** Certain investment products, such as bonds or dividend stocks, provide cash distributions to their investors on a regular basis. When putting money into your savings, consider investments such as these (either the direct securities or mutual funds or ETFs that hold these types of securities). Keep in mind, dividends and investment income are taxable as part of your annual income.

- **Don't buy stuff you don't need.** Someone had to say it.

## Finding Your Cash Flow Mojo

Now let's get back to our raison d'être, shall we? The purpose of all these ratios and ways of earning more, spending less and saving more of what you've got is to move you away from the nasty cash flow anxiety that sucks your energy, keeps you awake at night and turns you into a jittery, short-tempered stressed-out basket case, toward the cool, soothing, sexy vibe of cash flow mojo.

As we wrote in the Introduction, a positive cash flow is one of life's greatest luxuries. Certainly, it is the greatest monetary one. The confidence you gain when you have money in the bank to handle any emergency or to spend when opportunity knocks, well, to borrow from a certain credit card advertising campaign, it's priceless.

Money is a problem only when you don't have enough of it. But "having enough" is a concept entirely of your own making. It depends on the lifestyle you choose and the decisions you make about how you want to live. It is determined by the neighbourhood you reside in, the type of car you drive, the schools you send your kids to, the clothes you wear, the gifts you buy, the vacations you choose . . . the list is endless.

Every one of these lifestyle choices is also a financial decision. You can choose to live beyond your means, digging yourself and your family ever deeper into debt. Or, you can choose to live within your means, slowly tucking away cash and building your wealth. This book is for those who choose wealth. Choose cash flow, baby. Choose life!

## Five Steps to Positive Cash Flow

Every journey begins with a single step and your path to cash flow mojo starts right here! The first five steps are as follows:

1. Define your net monthly income—the amount *after* taxes and deductions. Add any other income you regularly receive each month.

2. Define your monthly expenses. Pull out your bank and credit card statements. Add up all the money you have spent. This is more than just debt servicing: this includes your shampoo, your gym fees, the school fees, the parking tickets, you name it. Get it in there.

3. Compare the two figures. Make adjustments so that income exceeds expenses. (Hint: earn more, spend less.) Take note of what you decide to cut out on the expenses side and/or what you need to add on the income side.

**4.** With more income than expenses, take the difference you've created (*that's surplus cash, baby!*) and use a large portion of it (say 80 per cent) to pay off any short-term debt (credit cards, demand loans); put the remaining amount into savings. Yes, you can pay down debt and save at the same time! Once your short-term debt is cleared, apply the difference to pay down long-term debt and keep saving.

**5.** Repeat monthly. Forever.

# 2

## Pay the Minimum—on Everything

*Take a look at your credit card statement. It should tell you how long it will take you to pay off the balance if you make the minimum payment. Shoot for a time frame that's longer than you can ever imagine living. That should do it. Now go have fun!*

### The Almighty Credit Card

Credit cards are magical. Whoever invented them should be given a Nobel Prize. You merely hand over this slim piece of plastic and, just like that, you can have anything you want. Brilliant! You can go wherever you like, buy as much as you wish and then, at the end of the month, you get a tasteful brown paper envelope in the mail with a little slip of paper inside explaining how much you owe. Wait a minute! *What?* You have to pay? Didn't the credit card take care of that? Where do they expect you will get the money for all this?

## How We Got into This Mess

Think back to your first credit card. Do you remember how you felt when you first held it in your hands? Were you proud? Nervous? Thrilled? Bored? You probably felt a little more mature, a little more responsible and a little more initiated into the adult world. How long was it before you realized you could pay for the trip to Vegas and put all the beers on your card and your buddies would pay you their share in cash? Sweet adulthood indeed.

And do you remember how you felt the first time a department store clerk or restaurant cashier looked at you with pity and explained that the credit card company had instructed them to cut up your card? Well, it was hardly your fault. The crazy folks at the bank were the ones who chose to give you the darn thing in the first place. They ought to be the ones held responsible, no?

## What Do Credit Card Companies Think of You, Anyway?

Credit card companies view their cardholders as members of various customer segments. While these may not be the *official* categories, see if you can recognize yourself in any of them:

- **The Goody-Goods.** These people are the least profitable for the credit card companies, because they pay their balance in full, on-time, every month. While the credit card issuer isn't able to collect interest from these people, rest assured they still make money on the transaction charges they collect from merchants. So even if the Goody-Good has the kind of card that pays him 1 per cent cashback on his purchases, the card company can still reap 3 per cent from the store where GG shops. While the GG's fiscal diligence might be obnoxious to his friends, GGs are like the nerds in high school. They pay attention to how stuff works, they do their homework and end up retiring early in order to manage their immense wealth from laptops on the terraces of their sprawling oceanfront villas. So geeky, right? According to the statistics held by the Canadian Bankers Association, two-thirds of Canadians fall into this category.[1] (The paying-off-their-balance category, not the geeky part.)

- **The Revolvers.** We call these people Revolvers, not only because they revolve their credit from one month into the next, but also because they are the customers around whom the credit card industry revolves. Revolvers always carry a balance and only pay enough to keep their credit card functioning. The many, many dollars of interest that revolvers pay are what keep credit card company employees showing up for work every day—and keep credit card company shareholders happy. About a third of Canadians are Revolvers, according to Canadian Bankers Association data.

- **The Defaulters.** When Revolvers lose control or an unforeseen crisis happens and they can't go on revolving anymore, they may become Defaulters. There are also less-than-honest people who willingly sign up for credit, sometimes fraudulently, with every intention of defaulting. The reason credit card companies charge such high fees and interest rates is because of the level of risk they take—trusting us to use their cards and then pay them the money we owe. According to the Canadian Bankers Association, credit card defaults are half as common in Canada as they are in the United States and in 2012 represented less than 1 per cent of credit card accounts. In the long aftermath of the 2008 financial crisis,

---

[1] Canadian Bankers Association, "Household Borrowing in Canada," CBA website, August 28, 2012, http://www.cba.ca/en/media-room/50-backgrounders-on-banking-issues/548-household-borrowing-in-canada.

the default rate on credit cards in Canada rose to as high as 1.34 per cent in January 2010.[2] In the United States, defaults were three times more common.

## Are You in Debt Denial?

If you are like most Canadians, you firmly believe your credit card debt really isn't so bad. While you might have a little ol' balance hanging around, it's nothing to be concerned about, right? You know whatever debt you've got can't possibly be as bad as those irresponsible spendthrifts you call friends, colleagues and family.

If you are among the two-thirds of Canadian Goody-Goods, paying off your balance in full and on time, then perhaps you are correct and you have no problem with the level of debt you regularly rack up on your credit card. However, if you are part of the other one-third of Canadian Revolvers (and there is a good chance you are, as a reader of this book), then you need to be clear about how much debt is too much for you—or risk ending up as a Defaulter.

A 2012 survey by www.RateSupermarket.ca found that 61 per cent of Canadians believe they have less debt than the average Canadian.[3] Since that is statistically impossible, it seems we might have just found our common national characteristic: debt denial.

In reality, the average amount of credit card debt is $3,277.33.[4] Forty-one per cent of Canadians have credit card debt of more than $3,000 and 25.5 per cent have more than $5,000. Another 10 per cent have more than $10,000 of credit card debt.

[2] Research Data Services, Canadian Bankers Association, "Credit Card Delinquency and Loss Statistics," CBA website, September 20, 2012, http://www.cba.ca/contents/files/statistics/stat_creditcarddelinquency_en.pdf.

[3] Ratesupermarket.ca, "Are Canadians in Credit Card Debt Denial?" *Infographics* (website), February 2012, http://www.infographicsarchive.com/economics/are-canadians-in-credit-card-debt-denial.

[4] Ibid.

The study went on to point out that, "of those that have over $11,000 in credit card debt, 17% think they have *less* debt than the average Canadian and 43% think they have the *average* amount of credit card debt."[5] So you see, no matter who you are, you think you are normal.

Clearly, those carrying $3,000 or more of credit card debt seem to think it's perfectly reasonable to do so. But from a Revolver perspective, let's look at what happens to $3,000 worth of credit card debt over time.

## How Much Is Your $3,000 Worth?

The Financial Consumer Agency of Canada has a nifty calculator on its website,[6] which allows you to calculate exactly how long it will take you to pay off that $3,000, and how much interest you will pay for the pleasure. We have reproduced a sample calculation below for your convenience.

Of course, there is one major underlying premise to the following calculation: we must assume that while paying off this debt, you will not be making further purchases on the card, which, as we know, is a pretty unlikely scenario given that 61 per cent of you think it's no biggie to be walking around owing $3,000 on your card. Anyhoo . . .

Most credit cards require a minimum monthly payment of between 2 and 3 per cent of the outstanding balance. On a $3,000 balance, that would cost $60–$90 each month. Well heck, you can afford that, so why *wouldn't* you keep paying the monthly minimum for, like, ever? Well, there is that little matter of the interest rate

---

[5] Ibid.

[6] Finance Consumer Agency of Canada, "Credit Card Payment Calculator Tool," FCAC website, 2011/05/04, http://www.fcac-acfc.gc.ca/iTools-iOutils/CreditCardPaymentCalculator/CreditCardCalculatorCalculate-eng.aspx.

on credit cards—typically between 18 and 21 per cent. Here's what that scenario would look like on balances between $1,000 and $10,000. (Note, we are assuming a 3 per cent minimum monthly payment, a 19 per cent interest rate and no interim spending on the card.)

As you can see, if you were to take everything you bought on your credit card and *doubled* the price, that's roughly how much you would end up spending if you only paid the minimum monthly balance on your credit card. Plus a little more. Were those shoes really worth double what you paid? Would you have paid double for that round of golf?

---

 **PAY TWICE AS MUCH? WHY NOT?**

You probably end up paying far more for your credit card purchases more often than you realize. And not just due to interest charges. Unfortunately, the only person to blame is the one holding the plastic. As a *Time* magazine article pointed out, "There are piles of evidence that people are bad decision makers when it comes to how they use their credit cards." A study by the Massachusetts Institute of Technology found that "people were willing to pay twice as much for basketball tickets when they were using a credit card as opposed to paying cash. Credit-card spending just doesn't feel like real money."[7]

---

## Going Above and Beyond

In Table 2.1, as long as you're not adding new purchases, each month the balance is reduced and therefore the amount of interest diminishes. If, however, you *continue* to use the card while only making

---

[7] Barbara Kiviat, "The Real Problem with Credit Cards: The Cardholders," *Time* magazine, May 12, 2009, http://www.time.com/time/business/article/0,8599,1897362,00.html.

**Table 2.1:** What you pay in interest on your credit card balance

| Original balance | $1000 | $3000 | $5000 | $10,000 |
|---|---|---|---|---|
| Minimum monthly payment | $30 | $90 | $150 | $300 |
| Time to pay off | 10 years and 5 months | 16 years and 10 months | 19 years and 10 months | 23 years and 11 months |
| Interest you would pay | $889.40 | $3,124.69 | $5,359.98 | $10,948.20 |
| Total amount you would pay | $1,889.40 | $6,124.69 | $10,359.58 | $20,948.20 |

minimum monthly payments, things get even more expensive, because each month the interest will be charged on the basis of your non-shrinking balance. If you can stop yourself from using the card while paying off the balance, Table 2.2 illustrates five scenarios that demonstrate the big difference you can make by going *above and beyond* that minimum monthly payment. (C'mon, you can do it!)

**Table 2.2:** The importance of paying more than the monthly minimum

| | You make only the minimum payment | You make the minimum payment *plus* $50 each month | You make the minimum payment *plus* $100 each month | You pay a flat amount of $100 each month | You pay a flat amount of $250 each month |
|---|---|---|---|---|---|
| Original balance | $3,000 | $3,000 | $3,000 | $3,000 | $3,000 |
| Interest to pay | $3,124.69 | $942.83 | $578.63 | $1,101.77 | $353.92 |
| Time to pay off | 16 years and 10 months | 3 years and 7 months | 2 years and 1 month | 3 years and 6 months | 1 year and 2 months |
| Total you pay | $6,124.69 | $3,942.83 | $3,578.63 | $4,101.77 | $3,353.92 |

You can also see how important it is to pay attention to that minimum amount, rather than just throwing a random lump sum at your account and assuming it's enough. (We're sticking with the example of $3,000 credit card debt with the same interest rate and minimum payment as in Table 2.1.)[8]

Hmmm . . . 16 years or 14 months? Obviously, the more of your balance you can pay off upfront and avoid compound interest charges, the better off you'll be financially. As we show in Chapter 3, compound interest is your best friend when it comes to your savings. When it comes to what you owe, however, interest is more like your nastiest ex: it just keeps piling up insults on top of injuries.

The only way to avoid this interest trap is to pay off your balance, in full, each month, and avoid interest charges altogether. The credit card companies may be a bit disappointed if they miss out on the chance to charge you interest—but you will have outsmarted them at their game. And as for your ex's drama, well, that's a subject for another book.

### Don't Be a Hater

Of course, there are two sides to every story. Credit cards aren't all bad (if used properly, Miss Goody Two-Shoes). Apart from the huge convenience of being able to pay quickly without having to worry about counting out change, credit cards provide a reliable online track record of all your purchases and payments. Here are just a few more of their redeeming qualities:

- **Safety and reliability.** Credit cards provide important advantages when it comes to your money (buyer protection and

---

[8] Finance Consumer Agency of Canada, "Credit Card Payment Calculator Tool," FCAC website, April 5, 2011, http://www.fcac-acfc.gc.ca/iTools-iOutils/CreditCardPaymentCalculator/CreditCardCalculatorCalculate-eng.aspx.

purchase assurance are two examples), but especially when travelling in foreign countries.

- **Grace periods.** Until your payment due date, the money you've borrowed on your credit card is essentially free. Your cash can remain tucked away in a high-interest savings account while you spend away on your credit card. Come payment time, you transfer your cash to the card, paying off the balance and never paying interest—only earning it. How gracious is that?

- **Cashback.** Many companies offer credit cards that provide a cashback incentive of up to 1 per cent, 2 per cent, or in some cases even 3 per cent on purchases you make using the card. In our minds, there is no better perk than cold, hard cash.

- **Reward points.** If you do a lot of spending on your card, reward points can really add up, giving you the chance to earn free flights, car rentals, restaurant meals and so forth. However, beware the annual fee for reward cards and make sure you're not paying for more than you earn.

- **VIP perks.** For those who like to roll like Kim and Kanye, certain prestige credit cards offer services such as private concierges and line-skipping privileges everywhere from rock concerts to the airport. Again, ask yourself: Are the perks worth the annual fee you pay?

- **Balance shifting.** Credit cards with lower interest rates can be useful if they also allow you to shift your balance over from higher-rate cards, although the rates are usually still higher than personal lines of credit. If you must carry a balance, at least let it be at the lowest possible rate of interest.

In the end, credit cards are like life: they are what you make of them. Personal responsibility should dictate that buying stuff on credit means actually having the money to pay for those items (and, as a bonus, earn a sweet reward for doing so). They can indeed be a valuable budgeting tool (hello travel points and buyer protection!), but they do need to be used responsibly. For those teetering on the less-than-fiscally-sound side, we propose a warning slapped on them: "This will cost you double, unless used responsibly."

---

**🔑 GOLDEN RULE: DID YOU FALL FOR A TEASE?**

What do you think: a low introductory rate of 4.9 per cent for six months or a slightly higher introductory rate of 7.9 per cent for 12 months? Assuming both would jump to a permanent 16 per cent interest rate after the introductory phase, which card would you choose? Academics at the University of Maryland found that most people chose the "'teaser'" rate of 4.9 per cent—which makes sense, right? It sounds like a better deal. However, it's only a better deal if your balance is paid off within the first six months. According to *Time* magazine, "As a species we're just really bad at understanding costs that come later on . . . We lock eyes with that initial low rate and can't look away."[9]

---

## A Word on Low-Interest Rate Cards

If one credit card has a 19 per cent interest rate and another has a 12 per cent interest rate, it's a no-brainer, right? Lower interest rates are always better? Not always. It depends what other fees are involved with the credit card in question—and as the Golden Rule above illustrates—what your balance habits are.

---

[9] Barbara Kiviat, "The Real Problem with Credit Cards: The Cardholders," *Time* magazine, May 12, 2009, http://www.time.com/time/business/article/0,8599,1897362,00.html.

**Table 2.3:** Comparing the cost of interest and annual fees while carrying a modest balance

| Balance owing | Interest charge | Annual fee | Annual cost (fees and interest) |
|:---:|:---:|:---:|:---:|
| $500 | $95 (19%) | $0 | $95 |
| $500 | $60 (12%) | $50 | $110 |

The Financial Consumer Agency of Canada[10] uses this example, which we think illustrates the point quite nicely. Imagine you are carrying a balance of $500. Table 2.3 shows what that might look like with a 19 per cent interest, no-fee credit card compared to a low-rate 12 per cent interest rate credit card that charges a $50 annual fee. (Note that the annual cost in the chart does *not* include paying the actual balance.)

As you can see in Table 2.3, the regular-rate card ends up being $15 cheaper, because the fee added onto the lower-rate card offsets any interest savings. However, watch what happens (Table 2.4) when you owe $3,000 instead of $500:

**Table 2.4:** Comparing the cost of interest and annual fees while carrying a larger balance

| Balance owing | Interest charge | Annual fee | Annual cost (fees and interest) |
|:---:|:---:|:---:|:---:|
| $3,000 | $570 (19%) | $0 | $570 |
| $3,000 | $360 (12%) | $50 | $410 |

With a larger balance, the lower-interest-rate card becomes the better deal—providing $140 in savings. In general, the larger your balance and the longer you carry that balance, the more impact the

---

[10] Finance Consumer Agency of Canada, "Choosing the Right Credit Card for You," FCAC website, November 8, 2012, http://www.fcac-acfc.gc.ca/eng/resources/publications/paymentoptions/RightCC/RightCC-3-eng.asp.

interest rate will have on what you owe. Either way, that's still a lot of money going to interest and fees. Wouldn't you rather pay off the balance and save the $140 for more fun things?

---

**⚷ GOLDEN RULE: SHOP BEFORE YOU SHOP**

Credit card companies are master marketers and there are so many different products, it can be overwhelming trying to find the right card with the right features for you. Generally speaking, there are three factors that distinguish credit cards from one another:

- Interest rates
- Additional fees and costs
- Rewards and benefits

Fortunately, the Financial Consumer Agency of Canada provides a Credit Card Selector Tool[11] on its website, www.fcac-acfc.ca, giving you the chance to shop for and compare credit cards without ever leaving the comfort of your chaise longue and iPad.

---

## Dangerous Games

As we have said, credit cards, when used appropriately, are a super-convenient form of credit that can provide plenty of benefits and perks and even temporary interest-free access to spending power. However, there are a few forms of credit that we do not love. Why? All too often the use of them indicates that there is a larger issue going on with cash flow. All of them end up being very expensive,

---

[11] Finance Consumer Agency of Canada, "Credit Card Selector Tool," FCAC website, November 2, 2012, http://www.fcac-acfc.gc.ca/iTools-iOutils/creditcardselector/CreditCard-eng.aspx.

costing you more cash in the long run and potentially sending you into the death spiral of debt that leads to real trouble.

**We don't love credit card cash advances.** When you withdraw a cash advance from your credit card, you are charged interest from *that moment* until the day you repay *the entire amount.* There is no grace period as there is with purchases. Sometimes the rate on cash advances is even higher than it is for purchases, so check the fine print.

**We don't love overdraft protection.** Like the kind of "protection" you see in gangster movies, overdrafts on your chequing account come at a very high price. First there is the monthly fee you pay for the *potential* of using it—often around $5 each month. Then there is the steep interest rate you pay on whatever you withdraw—sometimes 20 per cent or more—often higher even than your credit card rate of interest.

**We don't love payday loans.** As we discussed in Chapter 1, not only do payday loans suck up a huge portion of your upcoming cash flow (your next paycheque), they also eat up even more of your precious cash with shockingly high interest rates and fees, setting you back even further until the payday after the next payday. Stop this train, you want to get off!

**We don't love buy now, pay later.** Store credit that allows you to buy now with no money down and no interest is always too good to be true. This is a payment plan with myriad hidden dangers. Two examples:

- Suppose you apply for a $1,600 credit on the basis of a $1,557 purchase. Before leaving the store, you agree to a store warranty or a delivery fee, and suddenly the balance is $1,602.45. While you think, *it's just a couple dollars, no big deal,* the credit bureau (which sees all!) views your account as "over limit." For the next 24 or 36 months of "no pay, no interest," or until you pay off the balance, your credit report will retain this black mark against it.

• What if stuff happens and, when the 24-month no-pay period comes to an end, you don't have the cash to pay the full balance owing? No problem, the store will simply start charging you interest—retroactive to the day you signed the agreement *two years* ago. The interest rate will likely be in the astronomical 30 per cent range. If your original bill was $6,500, it could easily jump to more than $10,400 *the day after* your 24-month "free period" ends. Even if you start paying $500 a month, it will take you three more years to pay this off, and the eventual cost will grow to nearly $16,000. You call this a deal?

---

**GOLDEN RULE: CREDIT IS NOT CASH FLOW**

When you're trying to build some cash flow mojo, using credit to fund your cash flow crises can only set you back further due to the added costs of interest and fees. Emergency funds, savings accounts and relying on plain old cash when you're feeling constrained are all wiser solutions to handling a temporary crunch than piling on more debt. If you flat out don't have any of these resources, it's high time to pull out your statements, itemize where your spending is going, institute some serious cutbacks, create a monthly budget and start building those cash flow reserves. *Carpe diem—carpe pecunia* ("Seize the day—seize the money")!

---

## Hitting the Wall

When debt gets seriously out of control and the cash flow crises are blending into one another and there is no possibility of managing them anymore, sometimes there is no alternative but to wipe the slate clean and start over. If you are about to hit a financial wall, take a deep breath and trust us: there are solutions. They may be drastic, or they may be not quite as scary as you thought: it all depends on your level of debt and income. So let's start with the basics, and then look at your options.

## Checking Your Reputation

First things, first. We hate to get all schoolmarmish on you, but having access to credit is not a right, it is a privilege. By that, we mean credit is something you earn.

If you have no credit history, it can be a challenge to establish your credit-worthiness. You may have to start with a prepaid credit card, just to prove you can get the hang of spending and paying off a balance. Once you are finally granted your first credit card, it is up to you to start building your credit reputation.

Once you have your first credit card, department store card, personal line of credit or bank loan, everything you do credit-wise gets reported and shared with other financial institutions. A file on your credit history can be requested by any organization you seek credit from and even by your employers and landlords. How much you spend, whether you pay your balance on time and whether or not you stay within your limit—all this information is there for the viewing and judging. Yep, they all know your business. And you thought Facebook was bad.

## How to Check Your Own Credit

You look in the mirror before you head out the door, don't you? You want to make sure you're generally presentable before you face the world. Similarly, it is good practice to check in with the credit bureau every now and then to make sure everything is in order and that the way other institutions are viewing your credit is accurate and up-to-date. Here's how:

1. **Contact the credit bureaus.** Canada has two credit reporting agencies: Equifax and TransUnion. At least one or both will have credit reports on you. You can find their contact information and the process for requesting information on their websites at www.Equifax.ca and www.TransUnion.ca.

2. **Check your file.** Your credit report includes all your personal information, including addresses you've lived at, banking information, social insurance number, birthdate and so on. It will include information on any loans you have had, including how much, how long and your track record on paying them back. It will also include records of any late payments you've made to creditors, including utilities companies. Any people or organizations that have checked your credit will also be recorded.

3. **Clean it up.** It is very common for credit bureaus to have outdated or erroneous information and this will affect your credit reputation. Look for accounts that have been closed but still show as active and check for any misinformation about late or missed payments. Keep an eye out for any incidents of possible identity theft. If you've had a bad debt, it can be removed from your credit report, usually after seven years, but sometimes sooner.

## 50 Shades of Bankruptcy

No two personal financial situations are the same. Things that seem complicated to one person may be very simple to another. You may require third-party help to solve things or you may just need some direction in navigating to a better place. People find themselves in financial straits for all kinds of reasons: overspending, job loss, divorce, illness, business problems, gambling or family issues. However, following the financial crisis of 2008, there were more personal bankruptcy filings in 2009 than ever before—116,000 in Canada.[12]

Bankruptcy is a serious proceeding that should only be used as a last resort. In fact, even if you think you are a candidate, there are a number of options that might make sense for your situation:

- **Debt consolidation.** If you have a good job and therefore a steady source of income and your challenge is juggling several forms of high-interest debt, then debt consolidation may be the simplest answer for you. Debt consolidation loans are typically arranged through banks and credit unions. In some cases, a home equity line of credit (HELOC) might serve as the loan vehicle.

- **Credit counselling.** When in doubt, speak to an expert. Credit counsellors typically operate within non-profit organizations. They will look over your financial situation and make recommendations on how to best handle your immediate financial challenges and help you to create a budget for ongoing spending, saving and managing your debt.

- **Debt management plan.** If your situation requires it, a credit counsellor may contact your creditors on your behalf with a debt management plan. They will negotiate new terms to help settle your accounts within a reasonable time, while keeping you solvent.

---

[12] Office of the Superintendent of Bankruptcy Canada, "Statistics in Canada-2010," OSB website, July 31, 2012,  http://strategis.ic.gc.ca/eic/site/bsf-osb.nsf/eng/br02539.html.

- **Consumer Proposals.** This is similar to a debt management plan, with the difference that it is a formal, legally binding deal in which all your creditors are negotiated with and your debt is settled on your behalf. If half of your creditors accept the deal, then all are required to accept it, and they will have no future recourse against you. You then pay a portion of the overall debt over a maximum of five years.

- **Bankruptcy.** Filing personal bankruptcy gives you protection from your creditors. A licensed trustee administers the bankruptcy proceedings on your behalf. You make monthly payments, submit to credit counselling and you may lose some of your assets. Once the process is completed, however, you have a clean slate, though it may be difficult for you to obtain new credit right away.

Of course, we have only touched on the highlights of these solutions. All of them have ramifications with respect to your credit report. If your debt situation has become more than you can handle on your own and you think you could benefit from one of these solutions, then please get in touch with one of the many credit-counselling agencies in Canada as a first step.

## The Real Cost of Bankruptcy

Although many people think otherwise, bankruptcy is not a get-out-of-jail-free card. In fact, it is not even free. There are three major costs associated with a bankruptcy filing:

1. **Monthly payments.** Wait a second, you thought the whole purpose of filing for bankruptcy was to get out of monthly payments? Sorry to disappoint you! While a first consultation is free, the cost of hiring a bankruptcy trustee to administer your file is typically $200–$250 per month.

2. **Surplus income payments.** Based on how much you earn, the size of your family and other personal factors, the government will determine how much you can keep for living expenses. Any surplus income must then be handed over to the government.

3. **Non-exempt assets.** Any RRSP money you've contributed over the previous year, any tax refunds, HST credits and any equity in your home or car become the property of the estate in bankruptcy. Depending on your provincial rules and your situation, you may have the option of keeping your home or "buying" it back from the bankruptcy estate.

Each case is different, so it's best to discuss your options with a local trustee before deciding which route is best for you.

---

 **SEVEN YEARS OF BAD LUCK?**

Save it for the broken mirrors. While a bankruptcy filing or consumer proposal will negatively affect your credit rating for at least six or seven years (depending on where you live), in some cases you can begin repairing your credit reputation immediately. Secured credit cards—which you pay into and then use (like a debit card)—are ideal for the purpose of mending a broken credit report. Depending on your circumstances, you could be back on the right track again within 12 to 18 months.

---

## A Fresh New Start

There is no doubt that bankruptcy is a dramatic procedure. However, it is not the end of the world. In fact, it can be a life-altering way to end a situation that is out of control and allow you to make a healthy new start. Want some inspiration—or maybe just some consolation? These celebrities have all gone bankrupt and lived to see another day:

- Donald Trump: corporate bankruptcy in 1991, 1992, 2004 and 2009 (we're hoping 2013 isn't next)
- Larry King: personal bankruptcy in 1978
- Cyndi Lauper: personal bankruptcy in 1981
- Meat Loaf: personal bankruptcy in 1983
- Toni Braxton: personal bankruptcy in 2010
- Betsey Johnson: corporate bankruptcy in 2012
- Willie Nelson: personal bankruptcy in 1990
- Elton John: personal bankruptcy in 2002

But these celebrities have nothing to do with me, you protest! True, but their financial troubles are a clear indication that wealth has very little to do with income, and very much to do with cash flow and responsible spending and borrowing behaviour. If the queen of 1980s pop music can fess up to her true colours (I guess girls really do just want to have fun?), so, my dear, can you.

# 3

## Spend It All

*Financial advisers tend to recommend that you save up for things you want. That's impractical if you want things right now—now isn't it?*

Step right up, ladies and gentlemen, and take a ride in our time machine. We are taking you on a trip back to the late 1960s, a time when scientists at Stanford University were conducting cruel and unusual experiments on four-year-old children, using—wait for it—marshmallows. (What?)

The marshmallow test was (and still is) a behavioural psychology experiment to measure a child's ability to delay gratification. In the original test, a single marshmallow was placed on the table in front of each child. The kids were told they could eat the marshmallow immediately, or wait until the nice test lady returned in 15 minutes, at which time they would be given a second marshmallow. One now or *two* later. Hmmm... The nice test lady then closed the door, leaving each kid alone with a marshmallow and an agonizing decision.

For a kid facing a marshmallow, 15 minutes is an eternity. The kids squirmed, sniffed, poked. They talked to the marshmallow, they talked to themselves. Now, if you have kids of your own (or nieces, nephews, annoying small neighbours), think of what they'd do...

A few kids succumbed to the treat immediately (middle child, *cough*), a few more held out for several minutes before giving in and about a third managed to hold out for the second marshmallow. Those who were able to delay their gratification did so primarily by distracting themselves: they stared in another direction, kicked the table or covered their eyes. They found ways to pass the time while waiting as patiently as possible for their double marshmallow prize.

But the really interesting part is what happened when the academics checked in with those kids 20 and 30 years later. Turns out the ones who waited for the second marshmallow were better socialized as adolescents, ended up with better SAT scores and carried their ability to resist temptation in favour of long-term goals right into adulthood.[1]

In a similar study at Duke University, a professor of psychology and neuroscience tracked 1,000 people from the age of three to 38. She also found that the immediate marshmallow-eaters had trouble delaying gratification even as adults. One of her participants remarked: "Believe me, I understand all about saving for retirement, but I haven't saved any money because when I see a hot motorcycle, I buy it!"[2]

Sound familiar?

---

[1] W. Mischel, Y. Shoda, et al., "Behavioral and Neural Correlates of Delay of Gratification 40 Years Later," *Proceedings of the National Academy of Sciences*, Vol. 108, No. 36, August 29, 2011, http://www.pnas.org/content/108/36/14998.full.

[2] Maia Szalavitz, "The Secrets of Self-Control: The Marshmallow Test 40 Years Later," *Time* magazine, September 6, 2011, http://healthland.time.com/2011/09/06/the-secrets-of-self-control-the-marshmallow-test-40-years-later/marshmallow-test-40-years-later/marshmallow-test-40-years-later.

While we may be old enough to resist the appeal of a marshmallow, many of us succumb to the exact same desire for instant gratification on a daily basis, when, for example, we pull out our credit cards for a treat we can't afford, when we mortgage a huge house with almost no down payment, or when we throw caution to the wind and spend every penny we earn. In these cases, we behave as if there is no future; there's only today, right now, and the sweet rush of getting what we want, when we want it.

## Doomed to Instant Gratification?

Think you may be doomed to a life without savings because of that marshmallow you scarfed down at preschool? Further research at Duke University found that there are some traits, such as an individual's IQ, that change very little throughout a person's life. However, many people's self-control improves as they mature. So before you blame your genes for your propensity to blow your budget, remember that *you always have the choice* to delay gratification and focus instead on your long-term goals. So reach for those goals (and not for the peanut butter marshmallow square)!

## Waiting for the Money

But, seriously (we hear you asking), what does money have to do with marshmallows? If you're good and save your money instead of spending it immediately, well, it isn't as if some nice test lady is going to walk in and give you more cash, right?

Well, not exactly, but close. If you spend your cash, it's gone. If you save your cash in an interest-bearing account, that cash gets more valuable—turning itself into more and more cash the longer you wait. The reason is compound interest—and the more time you give it, the better it works.

## Time Is on Your Side

Oh, we know! Who has time for anything anymore? Time passes too quickly and we are always wishing we had more of it. Time can also be hard on us, stressing us out and making us lose our energy, our youthful looks, perhaps even our marbles. (*Oy vey!*)

However, when it comes to our money, time is like that nice test lady. Just set aside a portion of your money in an investment account, then sit back and simply watch it (don't touch it). Look away, hum to yourself, kick the table if you must! Resist the urge to spend it. Eventually, the kind lady of time will wave her magic wand of compound interest, dividends or growth, and reward you with more money!

Yes, time will turn your babies into teenagers and make those smooth, rosy cheeks of yours a web of little laugh lines. However, she will also make you a lot richer—if you let her.

## The Power of Compound Interest

Let's take a look at an example, shall we? Retirement savings—so boring, right? So far off in the future and so very *not* immediately gratifying. No wonder half of Canadians put off planning for retirement. Yet because of its long-term nature, saving for retirement is one of the best illustrations of how compound interest can make you so much wealthier, just by starting earlier and not eating that damn marshmallow.

We begin with two people: Patient Pat and Marsha the Marshmallow Eater. Pat starts saving for retirement at the age of 21 and makes a habit of putting $3,000 away in retirement savings every year. Marsha, on the other hand, can't imagine how she could live without that $3,000 to spend on clothes and iThings, so she eats marshmallows until she is 28, and then begins saving for retirement. Still, you think, 28, that's pretty good, right? How much difference could seven years in their twenties make (besides a cute little marshmallow muffin top)?

For the sake of simplicity, let's say Pat and Marsha both earn 8 per cent interest on their investments every year. Table 3.1 shows how much they would each have in their savings account, year after year:

Yes, Patient Pat has become a millionaire—on just $3,000 a year! Marsha has done well, but at 65, Pat will have $498,569 more in the bank than Marsha, even though Pat only came up with an extra $21,000 in cash. Marsha better hope that Pat will be buying the rounds at the golf club.

**Table 3.1:** The sooner the better

| Age | Patient Pat | Marsha the Marshmallow Eater |
|-----|-------------|------------------------------|
| 21 | $3,000 | |
| 22 | $6,240 | |
| 23 | $9,739 | |
| 24 | $13,518 | |
| 25 | $17,600 | |
| 26 | $22,008 | |
| 27 | $26,768 | |
| 28 | $31,910 | $3,000 |
| 29 | $37,463 | $6,240 |
| 30 | $43,460 | $9,739 |
| 40 | $137,286 | $64,486 |
| 50 | $339,850 | $182,680 |
| 60 | $777,170 | $437,852 |
| 65 | $1,156,517 | $657,948 |

The secret here is that Pat used those early years to get the compound interest party started. Interest grew not only on every new investment of $3,000, but also on the interest already accumulated. Interest upon interest. Compounding over time. Get it? You reading our mail, here?

## Money and Marshmallows

No one likes to think about getting old, and for those who are a long way from retirement, it can be hard to even imagine grey hair, not to mention a weekday that doesn't involve work. And, as we know from the kids in the marshmallow experiment, waiting is just plain hard, whether you're four years old or 40.

The decisions you make about your money every day are a lot more complicated than choosing whether or not to eat a sweet treat, yet the principle is the same: what you consume now has a future cost, and in many cases, it's one you really can't afford.

## So How Much Are We Talking Here?

Right. In an ideal world, where you had tons of income and no debt and could sock away thousands of dollars each month, we'd have you saving for all kinds of scenarios. However, we all live within certain financial parameters, such as limited earnings and monthly financial obligations that eat up our paycheques. As a result, we need to set attainable goals and prioritize what we are saving for at any given time.

So let's start with how much you can reasonably save each month. Back in Chapter 1, we asked you to calculate your savings rate to determine what percentage of your income is currently going toward savings. If you are not currently saving anything, then we suggested you aim for the industry standard of 10 per cent of your gross income. Take your monthly income and multiply by 0.10. This will tell you how much you need to set aside each month in order to achieve a 10 per cent savings rate.

Depending on your personal circumstances, you may be able to save more than 10 per cent (cue the applause!) or choose to save less. As long as you are doing the best you can (and we do mean the absolute best ... not some half-baked best) and doing it *regularly*—see the advice on automatic withdrawals in Chapter 1—it will become a habit, of the most highly effective kind.

---

**⚷ GOLDEN RULE: YOU CAN ELIMINATE DEBT AND SAVE AT THE SAME TIME**

Debt reduction can sometimes feel like an all-or-nothing proposition for many people: they feel as though they can't make progress and start saving until their credit card debt has been eliminated. Our thought is to take a more balanced approach. That is, allocate a certain amount that you can afford to do without each month and steer a portion of that toward debt reduction, and then put the remaining amount into savings. In this way, you are slowly paying down your debt and building up a valuable cash reserve at the same time. Now, why is this important when you're still carrying debt?

Well, if you have an emergency or an immediate need for cash, your cash reserve means that you'll have backup and won't need to rely on your credit card *again*. The psychology of this strategy is also key. You will now have the ability to create the habit of saving from the get-go, feeling the comfy security of having that cash reserve available when you need it, and (bonus!) continuing to feel the sense of accomplishment that comes from seeing a declining balance on your credit card statement. (Kinda like watching that scale go down every week while improving your jogging mileage at the same time. Doing them together leads to big long-term rewards.)

## So Much to Save for—Where Do I Start?

Once you've determined how much you can comfortably (or uncomfortably) save each month, what will you do with the money? Here are the primary types of savings plans a healthy household should have, categorized in order of savings priority and what you need to do with the funds once you've boldly—and wisely—agreed to save 'em (not spend 'em):

### 1. Emergency Fund

As we discussed in Chapter 1, this is your first priority. You need to have enough cash stashed away to cover at least three months of your living expenses—six would be better. Because you never know. You could suddenly find yourself out of work or your house could be flooded or your mother-in-law could move in, or all of the above. In any kind of sudden unfortunate scenario, having a cushion of cash will make you so grateful, you will immediately send us an email to thank us (to which we'll respond, "We told you so!").

    **How to invest:** Keep it in cash, for example, by placing it in a high-interest savings account. If you think you might be tempted to use the funds for "a retail emergency," make sure the account is not linked to your everyday debit card. Set it up at a different financial institution with a different debit card that is locked away in a safe, rarely accessed place (say, your gym locker). Remember, this is for household emergencies only.

### 2. Short-Term Savings

Short-term savings include any big-ticket items that you plan to purchase or spend money on within a few months or a few years. Maybe you want to save for the down payment on a house?

Or save up to go back to school? How about taking six months off work and travelling through Asia? See...saving isn't always boring! Being a disciplined saver can make even your spending more fun and gratifying.

**How to invest:** Short-term savings should remain liquid, meaning you can easily access these funds when you need them, without paying taxes or penalties. Typically, this means putting your money into a non-registered account, such as a basic savings account or a non-registered investment account. However, TFSAs (tax-free savings accounts) are registered accounts that allow you to withdraw funds without penalty. As such, these also are appropriate for your short-term savings.

If you know you will need to use the savings within a year or two, your primary goal should be to keep the money safe and intact, so it's all there when you need it. As a result, you probably won't want to put these savings in equities or investments that could cause the value of your savings to swing radically either up or down. Keep your cash as straight-up cash in a high-interest savings account, or consider a money market fund, which is a fancy way of saying a fund made up of a bunch of different securities (such as bonds, treasury bills, etc.).

If you know you won't need the money for, say, three to five years, you can choose to invest in slightly higher-earning securities such as GICs, treasury bills or bonds that will provide a guaranteed return on the maturity date, timed to when you will need to access the funds.

### 3. Long-Term Savings

This is the kind of stuff you don't want to touch for 15 to 30 years, or more. We're talking retirement money (a.k.a. the golden nest egg), or saving for your kids' college education. Long-term savings require you to keep adding to the pot, little by little, ideally each and every year. You know, let compound interest and growth do its multiplying thing. You want to invest it with the aim of growing it for the future, rather than merely protecting it for the short term.

**How to invest:** Keep these funds in a registered tax-sheltered account, so as to avoid owing taxes on the investment as it grows. Registered retirement savings plans (RRSPs) are designed with this in mind. They also give you the immediate benefit (hello, marshmallow!) of a tax deduction every time you sock away more money into them. RRSPs also have stiff penalties in addition to the tax that is due if you withdraw your money prior to retiring, so this acts as a nice little deterrent to keep you on your long-term savings game. Keep your eye on the prize!

When it comes to your kids' education, registered education savings plans (RESPs) are helpful, both from a tax-sheltering point of view and for the free money (!) that the government will kick in as a partial matching program. Yes, free money! (We said that again, just so you wouldn't miss it—and miss out on this rather rarefied opportunity.)

Tax-free savings accounts (TFSAs) are also beneficial for the tax-free component, and provide another powerful vehicle to grow your savings tax-free over the long term. Unlike RRSP accounts, you are free to withdraw the money at any time, without penalty.

Within these registered accounts, you may invest your cash in whatever securities you like (not just savings, as the name implies). Your investing options include equities (stocks), fixed income (bonds), guaranteed income certificates (GICs), treasury bills, mutual funds, exchange-traded funds (ETFs) ... or simply cash. The longer you're able to leave the money to grow, the more risk/return you might be willing to take on. However, balance is always good. Like a balanced diet, a balanced portfolio means you have a little bit of everything ... and all things in moderation, please!

> ### 🔑 GOLDEN RULE: YOUR AGE IS YOUR BOND
>
> When it comes to a balanced portfolio, the relative weight you choose to give to stocks and bonds depends a lot on how comfortable you are with risk and your desire for potentially higher returns. When you are young, with many decades between you and retirement, you have more time to ride out the highs and lows of the stock market. As you get older and closer to the big retirement day, you will want to shift your investment mix more on the side of caution, protecting the gains you have made and making sure the money will be there when you need it. A rule of thumb is to weight your bonds with your age. So if you're 25, your portfolio might include 25 per cent bonds and 75 per cent equities. Once you turn 40, your portfolio would shift to include 40 per cent bonds and 60 per cent equities. Of course, a risk-averse 25-year-old and an aggressive 40-year-old might be happier to swap these portfolios.

## Excuses, Excuses

Finding reasons not to save is apparently a national pastime. In 2011, a Royal Bank of Canada survey revealed that nearly 40 per cent of Canadians admitted that they were saving less than in previous years. Furthermore, some 30 per cent of Canadians said they find it difficult to be disciplined about saving. There is no question that excuses are far easier to come by than good financial habits.

If you want to ensure a stable financial future for yourself and your family, you are going to have to toss those excuses in the trash and get yourself focused on a solid savings plan. Of course, old habits die hard (hello, beer gut!). So let's confront some of those tried-and-true excuses and see what you can do when the bad behaviour starts to creep back in ...

*Excuse #1: I Don't Know How to Save*

Really? Let's take a look in your closet, shall we? See any of those Cliff Huxtable–type sweaters from the late eighties lurking in there? How about the Club Monaco and Beaver Canoe–logo sweatshirts? And how many pairs of black shoes do you have? If you know how to collect, you know how to save. What if you could change your thought patterns and make a conscious effort to collect, say, dividends, instead of old ski jackets? You know how to do this: you just need to commit to collecting *cash* instead of *stuff*.

If you're convinced that you don't know how to save, start small and then stick to it. Maybe you could start with a savings jar: just drop in $20 (heck, even $5) every time you make a cash-machine withdrawal. Once you get in the habit of putting aside money rather than spending it, try and boost the amount you put aside each time. It's kind of like doing push-ups. At first you can only do a few (okay, three girly ones), but the more you do every day, the easier they'll get, and the more you'll be able to perform (*Look, Ma, no hands!*). The same goes with putting money aside. Flex that savings muscle!

*Excuse #2: I Don't Have Enough Money to Save Properly*

Thanks to the recent recession, many people have had to get used to earning less and making do. In the face of household cutbacks, the habit of saving is often abandoned. However, having too much *month* left at the end of your money still doesn't get you off the hook when it comes to saving. You still want to retire, don't you? You still need an emergency fund, right? Perhaps now more than ever.

So before you blame your paltry paycheque, take a good long look at all the little unnecessary places your money may be going. Look for ways to reduce your spending in order to free up some resources. You may think you are living on a razor-thin budget, but when you examine your daily habits, you'll almost always find there is more room than you expected.

### Excuse #3: I Don't Have the Time

Do you have 15 minutes? That's all it takes to set up an automatic withdrawal from your chequing account into your savings account or retirement fund. If you can make time to Skype with your friends or watch an episode of "Modern Family," you have enough time to set up an easy-peasy, no-brainer saving strategy. Fifteen minutes to peace of mind and a sounder financial future? Claire would make Phil do it!

### Excuse #4: I Don't Know How to Invest, It's Too Complicated

You don't have a degree in dentistry, but you do brush your teeth. You don't need to be a trained chef to make a tasty meal for your family. And not having your own real estate licence did not deter you from buying your first home, right?

Your personal finances are the same. There are a few simple rules we all need to get our heads around in order to realize the goals we hope to achieve. Saving does not mean you must invest in the stock market or get involved in a fancy financial plan. You can start with the basics and stop there, or you can keep learning and add things as you go. You can keep your finances as simple—or as sophisticated—as you wish.

Case in point: if technical financial terms and complicated investment products scare you away from saving, start with your friendly neighbourhood bank. At the most basic level, everything you need for setting up your savings plan is right there. The personal financial representatives at the bank are trained to help beginner savers and investors understand their options through the use of plain language and straightforward advice. Just go on in and start talking...

### Excuse #5: I Have Too Much Debt

Well, that may be true. If you're in debt, particularly credit card debt, you should definitely work at getting rid of it. However, it is that same discipline of building a habit—of taking a chunk of money every single month and applying it to your debt load—that will help you to kick-start your savings plan. As soon as your credit card is cleared (or at the same time, as suggested earlier in this chapter), keep up the glorious habit and apply that monthly sum to savings. So much more gratifying to build wealth than to pay for past purchases, no? Getting your emergency savings fund in place will be the first order of business, so that in the future you won't have to turn back to the ol' CC whenever an unexpected expense arises.

### Excuse #6: I'm Too Young to Worry About Saving

Oh, the glory of youth! Sorry to burst your bubble, kid, but there is no minimum age on a savings account. In fact, it's actually easier to save while you are young. You think your grocery bill is expensive now? When you don't have a family to support and you're not yet paying off a mortgage, your bills are relatively small. Now is the perfect time to build your wealth so saving becomes a habit. You can become that self-made millionaire you *just know* you're destined to be!

### Excuse #7: Interest Rates Are Too Low to Bother With

True, interest rates are at an historic low, but there are other easy-to-use, higher-return investments you could choose from, such as mutual funds and exchange-traded funds. They come in a whole spectrum of investing styles, many of which are low-risk and offer returns that are higher than the going interest rate.

With that said, don't dis basic cash savings accounts. Which will give you a better long-term return on your dollar: a 1.2 per cent interest rate or another night out with friends? Putting money in the bank gives you the confidence of cash flow mojo. Blowing your paycheque every week gives you a momentary high . . . and a lifetime of anxiety.

### Excuse #8: I Have an RRSP, So That's Good Enough

It is excellent that you are saving for your retirement. A very good thing, indeed. However, an RRSP is only part of the picture. What about the life that happens in all those years *before* you're ready to receive your senior's discount? An emergency fund will back you up during all those times in life when things do not go according to plan (you're 40 years old and just found out you need braces . . . *really?*). While a short-term savings plan will give you the means to take advantage of all those wonderful, often unexpected, opportunities that will surely come along. ("Disney World just went on sale . . . let's surprise the kids!")

### Excuse #9: My Partner Makes Enough to Take Care of Us Both

Having a main breadwinner is all well and good, until something happens, and he or she is no longer there to support you. We hate to sound like the purveyors of doom, but between divorce and widowhood, nearly all of us will find ourselves single at some point, and quite possibly not blessed with the lifestyle to which we have become accustomed.

Ultimately, each of us is accountable for our own financial situation. Claiming that you didn't know, or blaming someone else for the financial decisions that changed your life, won't bring back the opportunity to properly prepare yourself. The more you rely on someone else to control your financial well-being, the tougher it will be to figure things out and depend on *yourself* later on.

There are a number of variations on excuse #9, such as, "My kids will look after me when I'm old," and "My parents will leave me an inheritance when they die." To which our response is: "Have you seen your kids?" The point is, there's rarely enough money to go around. Kids have a funny way of making their own life choices, and parents have a way of running off and marrying someone half their age. Both have the potential of making investment decisions that may not be in *your* best interest. Plan accordingly.

### Excuse #10: I Can't Take It with Me

You're right about that! Let's hit Vegas! Okay, let's be honest: you're not always going to be young, healthy and eager to race into the office every morning. And you may just end up living a lot longer than you imagined. Having enough savings will make that last third of your life way more comfy and a heck of a lot more fun. If you're adamant about not leaving any inheritance behind, just think about the incredible hundredth birthday extravaganza you'll throw.

## A Million Dollars of Nothing

Now that we've talked you out of your excuses, we want to address the little ways in which you may be sabotaging your own best efforts to save. Even if you're smart and frugal about waiting until things go on sale and never paying retail, you probably don't think twice about spending smaller sums here, there and, well, everywhere. Why? Because it's easy and convenient. The problem is, these little expenses can add up to serious money—like *a million bucks* over your lifetime. Don't believe us? Read on ...

1. **Your daily brew.** You've probably heard about "the latte factor," but it's not only for those indulging in a daily Grande extra-whip Mocha Frappuccino. Suppose you buy a large coffee every morning. This will set you back about $2. That's $10 per week if you buy one every day on your way to work. At a 10 per cent rate of return (the average rate the TSX has returned over the past 20 years), investing that money could leave you with $56,000 in the bank after 25 years. Hmmm, maybe making coffee at home and dropping the toonie into a savings jar isn't so crazy. At about $15 per pound, your home brew will cost you mere pennies per cup.

2. **Lunch at work.** We know, packing a lunch can be a total drag. It's bad enough when you have to do it for the kids. Yet the average food-court lunch costs at least $7. Add it up over your working life and you will probably spend around $196,890 on crappy, high-sodium, high-calorie takeout food. Make it yourself, include the food you really like, and not only will you increase your cash flow mojo, you will probably end up healthier and slimmer. Richer *and* skinnier. Bada bing bada boom!

3. **Bank fees.** The average Canadian spends about $16.20 per month on bank fees.[3] That doesn't sound too bad, except when you consider that you are paying the bank to hold onto your money, which they then turn around and invest to earn a profit on. So why pay more fees than you have to? There are many accounts that cost much less. Some are even free. If you were to invest that money you are wasting on fees, it could net you more than $20,000 over your banking years. Who's the smart one now?

---

[3] Statistics Canada, Selected household expenditure items 2009, average monthly expenditure, http://www.cba.ca/en/media-room/50-backgrounders-on-banking-issues/82-banking-service-fees.

**4. The lottery.** The average Canadian spends $22.11 a month on lottery tickets[4] in the hope of striking it rich. Meanwhile, your odds of being hit by lightning while you're checking the numbers are actually much, much better. Furthermore, there's a reason we don't go around worrying about being hit by lightning—it's too unlikely to waste energy on. Unfortunately, winning the lottery is even rarer than lightning strikes. Invest your weekly $22 instead: after 25 years, you'll have $28,000 in the bank. Jackpot!

**5. Cable television.** Cutting the cable cord is a tough sell for a lot of people. But in your heart of hearts, you know it's a lot of money for a lot of wasted time. Suppose you pay $56 a month—and that's the low end in most parts of the country. That kind of money would give your savings a serious boost— to the tune of $73,000 if you were to invest it instead. With so much free content online and sites such as Netflix offering unlimited television and movies at a mere $8 or so a month, paying for cable starts to look pretty old-fashioned and darned expensive. Just think of how much more productive you'll be!

**6. Interest on your debt.** Yes, we know the interest on your debt is not exactly optional, but continuing to spend and rack up debt that you must then pay interest on is absolutely optional! The average Canadian has $25,960 in consumer debt.[5] Yikes! If this balance is on a credit card with an annual interest rate of at least 18 per cent, you could easily shell out more than $38,000 *in interest*—which is *so* unrewarding. Instead,

[4] Statistics Canada, Selected household expenditure items 2009, average monthly expenditure, http://www.cba.ca/en/media-room/50-backgrounders-on-banking-issues/ 82-banking-service-fees.

[5] Roma Luciw, "Average Canadian's Consumer Debt Hits $25,960," *The Globe and Mail*, February 23, 2012, http://www.theglobeandmail.com/globe-investor/personal-finance/ home-cents/average-canadians-consumer-debt-hits-25960/article548293.

spend that $38,000 by gradually putting it into your savings plan. Over a period of 25 years, you'll have amassed $163,000. Looks way better on you.

7. **Car lease.** Let's say you're conservative and you lease that cute but relatively modest $25,000 car. This will cost you about $400 per month. Not bad, right? Well…invest that money instead and you'll have—are you ready for it?—more than $519,272 in the bank after 25 years. Yup, half a million bucks, right there. More to the point, if you put aside $400 a month in savings, it would only take you about four years to save up $25,000, and you could go buy that sweet ride outright, *with cash*. You know, because that's just how you roll.

If you add up all these optional expenses and factor in a 10 per cent return, the fortune you coulda woulda shoulda had is roughly $1 million over 25 years. But even if you can only get a more modest 5 per cent return, you would still be able to reap $500,000. And these are just a few minor examples. We're quite sure you can find plenty of ways to trim small expenses that have little impact on your quality of life *now*, but could have a massive impact on the quality of your life *in the future*.

## The Sweet Taste of Self-Discipline

Life is full of temptation. We are certainly not suggesting that you need to cut out every indulgence that makes your life enjoyable in order to save every penny for the future. As we said earlier, balance is essential. The "'sweet spot'" comes from finding a way to enjoy the delectable things in life now, but also knowing when to exercise a little self-discipline. If a four-year-old can suffer through 15 minutes of self-denying torture in pursuit of something, well, *sweeter*, chances are you can do it too.

# 4

## Buy a Huge House

*Why have a smaller house when you can afford the mortgage payments on a bigger one? If you're lucky, the market will rise, giving you some extra equity to spend!*

Home sweet home. No other financial investment in your life will ever be as expensive or as emotional. Whether it's a house, a condo or a cottage, when a piece of real estate becomes your *home,* it is immediately invested with a whole truckload of ideas and biases that often reach right down to the core of your self-image.

Unlike your RRSPs, your mutual funds and your chequing accounts, where you choose to live can easily become a symbolic purchase, a reflection of how you want to present yourself to the world (and to the folks back home!). People fall in love with real estate. No wonder they get into bidding wars. No wonder so many homebuyers end up going over budget. Financial concerns go out the window and we let irrational emotions be our guide.

It is far too easy for your home—ideally a place of comfort and security—to become an overpriced, over-leveraged, stress-inducing status symbol. Choosing a home beyond your means creates cash flow anxiety and that awful condition known as "house poor." Of course, you want to love where you live. But if the extra bedrooms, heated tiles and chef-style kitchen end up squeezing your budget to the point where you can't pay your other bills, you can't save for your retirement and you can't even think about taking a vacation—then it's time to re-evaluate how much this home is contributing to your quality of life. A home needs to be comfortable—physically *and* financially. So let's figure out how to do that, shall we?

## How Much Are You Spending on Your Home Now?

Back in Chapter 1, we asked you to calculate your housing expense ratio, also known as your gross debt service ratio. This calculation tells you what percentage of your gross income is currently going toward housing. As a reminder, it goes like this:

$$\text{(Monthly housing costs} \div \text{monthly income)} \times 100$$
$$= \text{housing expense ratio}$$

You don't want this figure to exceed 32 per cent. If you are spending upward of 32 per cent, you are probably feeling the strain of keeping up with your payments every month. The lower your ratio, the more affordable your home is for you and the more cash flow mojo you have.

Of course, this ratio does not take into account all the other debt payments you may have racked up (for that, see "debt-to-income ratio" in Chapter 1). But even if you are very responsible and have no other debt, spending more than 32 per cent of your gross income on your housing is *just too much*.

## How Much Should You Be Spending?

We are so glad you asked. Take your gross monthly income (hopefully it's not too gross) and multiply it by 0.32. This is the top end of what you can comfortably afford—again, not taking into consideration what other credit card debt or outstanding loans you might have. The less you spend on housing, the more cash flow you will have left to spend on other things—such as feathering that nest.

We are also pretty sure there is a direct relationship between your housing expense ratio and your blood pressure, but science has yet to back us up on this.

---

**⚷ GOLDEN RULE: LIVE WITHIN YOUR MEANS!**

Who wants to do all that math, anyway? We do! Fire up the ol' interweb and check out our handy "Living within your means" online calculator on www.GoldenGirlFinance.com. Just fill in the blanks and we instantly tally up your ratios. You're welcome!

---

*Three Ways a House Is Like Any Other Investment . . .*

Sure, sure, you live in it, sleep in it, water its lawn . . . but let's not forget that your home is also a financial investment and, in that regard, you need to remember a few general rules common to all investments and how they apply to real estate specifically:

1. **To make money, you need to buy low and sell high.** Buying when prices are higher than ever before, or buying an overvalued home, will put you at greater risk of losing your investment if and when prices fall.

2. **Investing for the long term reduces your risk.** In any financial market, prices can bob up and down and sometimes recessions can cause them to stay down for a few years. Over the long term, however, prices generally rise due to the natural forces of inflation. Buying a house to live in for many years means that when you eventually decide to sell it, there is a much greater likelihood that the house will be worth more than what you paid for it.

3. **Paying fewer fees means more cash toward your investment.** The transaction costs of buying and selling a home can seriously eat into any potential you have for a profit—so find ways to reduce or avoid them. Real estate commissions, legal fees and moving costs can add up to 5–7 per cent of your home's purchase price, plus any potential mortgage penalties if you're selling one property to buy another. And don't forget to factor in the cost of property renovations and maintenance. With this in mind, buying a house to flip or that you only plan to live in for a couple of years gives you even less chance to recoup those costs while putting you at the mercy of any short-term market changes.

### ... And One Way a House Is a Very Different Kind of Investment

Most people buy a house by going into debt. While some people do borrow money to invest in their RRSP or the stock market, the majority of people use savings and available cash flow to fund their other investments. Conversely, you may say you own your house, but in reality *your bank* paid for it and owns most of it. The faster you pay off the bank (i.e., your mortgage), the sooner you will actually *own* your investment and the better chance you will have at pocketing some of that profit when it comes time to sell.

## Real Estate Prices Always Go Up, Right?

Many people in Canada can't remember a time when home prices weren't steadily on the rise. But when prices keep going up, how can you tell if the house you have your eye on is worth its asking price or if it is seriously overvalued? Pay attention to rental rates and you'll find your first clue. Here are a few ways to figure out if that home is "all that" or not:

- **Prices versus rents.** Check out what it costs to rent a comparable place and how rents have changed over the past few years in comparison to home prices. In a normal, equitably priced neighbourhood, house prices and rents should increase at the same rate, since they both depend on the demand for shelter in that community. However, when the cost of buying keeps going up while rents stay pretty much the same, this is a sign that people are feeling encouraged to buy homes due to "artificial" incentives—such as low interest rates and generous bank lending policies. As soon as interest rates rise or banks stop lending so readily, a lot of people will discover that buying in a particular neighbourhood is out of their league. With fewer buyers, prices will fall back.

- **Prices versus incomes.** Normally, when house prices are rising, incomes are rising too, since people have the means to take on bigger mortgages. Rising income also causes rents to rise, since people are feeling flush and are willing to pay more to rent the places they want. However, if rents are *not* rising and incomes are *not* rising—but house prices are still rising—it's a sign that all is not right in the economy. Homes in this scenario are most likely overvalued and poised for a correction.

- **Do the research.** Or, you could skip the private eye–type investigation and just check out the many statistics that analysts and economists are more than happy to provide. In 2011, *The Economist* magazine revealed that Canadian house prices were overvalued by 71 per cent relative to rents and 29 per cent relative to income.[1] Of course, these are national averages, so you do have to dig a little deeper to see what exactly is going on in your 'hood.

## Are You Building Equity or Paying Interest?

You've heard it a million times (perhaps from your father-in-law alone): Why throw away your money on rent when you could buy a home and build equity? In theory, this is true. The trouble is too many people buy a house thinking they will build equity and end up just paying a lot of interest to the bank.

A mortgage doesn't give you equity: a down payment is equity. Anything you pay toward the principal of your mortgage is equity. Paying the interest is just paying interest—there's no equity involved and you're no further ahead than if you were just paying rent.

### How Much Equity Do You Need?

Let's put it this way: the more equity you have, the better protected you are. If you have 10 per cent equity or less, you have entered the danger zone. You are among the most at risk of not being able to afford your mortgage payments and potentially of losing your home if interest rates rise by even 1 per cent.

But what if you have more than 10 per cent? Just how much is enough? Let's find out.

- **15 per cent equity or less: caution zone.** You are at risk of being stuck with negative equity in the event of a housing correction. As we write this, some analysts are expecting

---

[1] "House of Horrors, Part Two," *The Economist*, November 26, 2011, http://www.economist.com/node/21540231.

Vancouver and Toronto (especially condo owners) to experience a 15 per cent market correction over the next few years.

- **20 per cent equity or more: safety zone.** You have made a great start at building enough equity to protect you from falling prices *and* rising interest rates. Keep going! Make it a goal to *own* more than you *owe*.

 **WHAT IS NEGATIVE EQUITY?**

If you buy a house with a very small down payment and arrange for a long future of low monthly payments, you will end up paying a ton of nasty interest and you will have a hard time building any equity. If you sell your house to buy another, you could end up swapping one mortgage for another without making any profit. Worse, if your house price drops, it could become worth less than the outstanding mortgage *you still owe*. This is called "negative equity." If you had to sell, not only would you not make a profit, you would have to write a big cheque to the bank to make up the difference. *Quelle horreur!*

**GOLDEN RULE: ROOM TO WIGGLE**

When budgeting for a house purchase, make sure there is plenty of wiggle room in your budget. Just because you can afford the monthly payments doesn't mean you can afford the home. If you cannot get started with a 20 per cent down payment, you probably cannot afford to buy. If the monthly payments plus your other monthly debt payments exceed 40 per cent of your gross monthly income, (we'll say it again) you probably cannot afford to buy. If you push the limits anyway and buy a house that is too expensive for your budget, you will very likely end up living off your credit cards to get through each month. This is not the path to prosperity. It is the path to a big, gaping debt hole.

## Embrace Your Renting Side

For many people, buying a first home is a rite of passage. They see it as a necessary step toward becoming a mature adult and participating fully in the national economy. In some cultures, buying a home is a point of pride and renting can be seen as a social stigma.

We ask you, since when is getting into unsustainable debt a sign of maturity? How is putting your family's financial future at risk at all responsible? Do not buy into the hype of buying a home for appearance's sake or because your brother just bought a big house and your sister-in-law feels the need to remind you of this fact every day. Let your brother and his wife deal with their own heavily mortgaged conscience. Remember: the road to foreclosure hell is paved with real estate envy.

If you cannot come up with the cash for a 20 per cent down payment on the property you want—wait! Hold your fire. Consider renting while saving up more cash and in the meantime keep an eye out for falling prices and bargain properties. A more informed and prepared buyer makes a wiser purchase every time. Here is how you can determine whether it's the right time for you to buy or rent.

First, add up the monthly costs of owning the home you want. Include the following in this calculation: mortgage principal payments, interest charges, taxes, insurance and any other monthly payments such as utilities and condo fees. *Don't forget to account for upkeep.* The rule of thumb is 2 per cent of the home price per year, so divide this by 12 to get your monthly cost. (There is a reason homes are called "money pits"!)

Now figure out how much it would cost you to rent a similar property in the same neighbourhood. Check www.Kijiji.ca, www .Craigslist.ca and property rental sites. If you are working with a realtor, he or she also can provide you with rent statistics. Keep in mind, rent is usually negotiable depending on your willingness to sign a lease and on the quality of your credit and references.

If you can afford at least a 20 per cent down payment *and* the monthly mortgage payments will not exceed 32 per cent of your monthly income, then hook it up, you soon-to-be-homeowner, you! It sounds like you may have found your house match.

If, however, you find that renting would be much more economical for you at the current point in time, make sure you stick any available cash into a regular savings plan. That extra cash flow is your future nest egg. Nurture it carefully by putting it into a tax-free savings account where you can invest it and let it grow without penalty. Contribute to it monthly and soon you will have that beautiful big down payment that will allow you to buy the property of your dreams.

There is another possibility: maybe you would prefer to never buy a house and instead enjoy the flexibility of permanently renting. While many people love the idea of using their home as their primary investment vehicle for the long term, plenty of others prefer to invest their long-term savings in the stock market, in other types of real estate investments or in business ventures. There is no rule that says you must buy a home in order to succeed financially. Too many people have proven the opposite.

 **FORGET ABOUT TIMING THE MARKET**

Timing the market means keeping your eye on all the economic indicators so you can be sure to buy low and sell high. Market timing—in real estate and in stock market investing—is best left to the experts. For the average homebuyer, it is much less stressful to find a solid investment that you can live with for a long time and simply ride out the inevitable market fluctuations. Ultimately, buying a house is kind of like finding a spouse: you can sit on the sidelines forever and analyze every opportunity, but you'll be much happier if you just focus on what you love—and what you can afford—and then do your best to make it comfortable for the long term.

## The Five Cs of Borrowing

We know you are wonderful and *you* know you are rock-solid reliable, but are you wondering how a mortgage lender might size you up? Here are the five key criteria most banks and mortgage lenders look for:

1. **Capacity.** Is your income sufficient to make the mortgage payments once all your other debts are factored in? You can prepare for this by calculating your debt-to-income ratio (see Chapter 1) in advance and making sure it's below 40 per cent.

2. **Capital.** Size matters! The size of your down payment indicates how serious you are about investing and reduces risk all around. Twenty per cent shows you mean business.

3. **Collateral.** The lender will do a quality check on the property to make sure its value is worth the amount you want to borrow. Your realtor can provide you with comparables, but most lenders will have access to their own research.

4. **Character.** Despite your winning smile and great sense of humour, lenders really want to be sure you are a fine, upstanding, reliable member of the community. Bring evidence of your education, employment history and previous residences.

5. **Credit.** A lender will do a credit check on you by requesting a report from one of Canada's two credit bureaus, Equifax and TransUnion. The report provides a summary of your credit activity over the past six years. You can get ready by contacting the credit bureau in advance and making sure everything in your report is accurate and up-to-date, before the lender takes a look.

**WHAT IF YOU'RE NOT AN IDEAL CANDIDATE?**

Buck up, little camper. Nobody is perfect. Just because you may not meet all five Cs perfectly doesn't mean you can't qualify for a mortgage. Many lenders may be willing to accept you as they view you as a reasonable credit risk overall.

· **New to Canada?** Prove you have a steady job with reliable income or flex the muscle of your prominent down payment.

· **Self-employed?** If you can't demonstrate a regular income, show off your minimal debt load, your sterling credit history and your solid client contracts.

· **Credit mistakes?** When your credit history has a black mark or two, prove that you have your debts under control and you've taken steps to improve your rating. A strong, reliable income and a hefty down payment will certainly help your case.

## Finding the Perfect Mortgage

Finding the right home can take a long time and a lot of legwork. You trek through a myriad of open houses, scan weekly listings, peruse weekend show homes until you finally find the one place you can imagine coming home to, the one that you know you can customize just to your taste. But your decisions are not over: now you have to figure out what kind of mortgage you want. Here is a list of options you can consider to help make sure your mortgage fits as comfortably as your new home:

1. **Variable-rate mortgage.** For those who can handle a little uncertainty, variable-rate mortgages are often a better deal over the long term. With a variable-rate, the interest you pay

fluctuates in line with the lender's prime rate. With some loans, how much you pay each month rises and falls right along with interest rate. Alternatively, you pay the same amount each month and the portion that goes to interest rises as rate rises. If rates drop, less of your payment goes to interest and more is applied to equity. Typically, a variable-rate mortgage offers a lower rate overall than the equivalent loan with a fixed rate. There is also usually the option to switch to a fixed-rate mortgage at any time.

2. **Fixed-rate mortgage.** Locking in to a fixed-rate mortgage is like any sure thing: you pay a little more for the privilege of certainty. However, for many people, the advantages are worthwhile. For one thing, your rate is fixed for the entire term of the mortgage, so if rates are low when you sign the mortgage, you can be sure of keeping that rate until it's time to renew. Furthermore, you will always know exactly how much your payments will be and exactly how much interest you are paying versus how much equity you are building. If you are the kind of person who stays awake worrying about what interest rates will do, then by all means, a fixed rate might be the best option for you.

3. **Amortization.** This is the length of time it will take you to pay off the mortgage in full. Most first-time buyers choose a 25-year amortization. Shortening your amortization period will increase your payments, but more importantly, decrease the total interest you pay. Lengthening your amortization adds to the amount of interest you end up paying—increasing the cost of your home.

4. **Term.** No matter how long your amortization is, the time is broken up into terms. Your payment schedule and interest rate plan remain in force for the duration of each term.

A term could be six months, a year or as many as seven years. At the end of a term, you have the opportunity to renegotiate the payment schedule and the rates.

5. **Payment frequency.** How about never? Good try. You can choose from monthly, semi-monthly, weekly, biweekly or accelerated weekly/biweekly. The more frequent your payments, the more quickly your mortgage gets paid and the less interest you pay overall.

6. **Open or closed.** Suppose you suddenly get a miraculously awesome windfall and you want to pay off your mortgage and be done with it? An open mortgage allows you to do this without penalty. A closed mortgage means you are locked in until the end of your term. If you want to pay off the mortgage early, you can, but you will pay an extra fee for the pleasure.

7. **Paying it down.** Some mortgages will give you a once-a-year chance to pay down a portion of your principal. Seize this opportunity! Just do it.

---

**⚷ GOLDEN RULE: OWN IT**

We're talking about an attitude here. Taking the leap into owning real estate is no small commitment. So if you're going to be an owner—*own it*. Be as aggressive as you can about paying your mortgage down quickly so that you can own more and *owe less*. You chose to own rather than rent in order to build equity, right? So build it. Faster, sooner, better. If you take the slow, protracted route of minimal payments over a longer period of time, you will needlessly waste so much of your hard-earned cash on interest that you may as well have stuck with renting.

## Tax-Deductible Mortgages

Many first-time homebuyers want to know if mortgage interest payments are tax deductible. While our American cousins have this benefit, sadly, here in Canada, most of us do not. However, there are certain circumstances in which mortgage interest *can* be tax deductible. For example, if you borrow against your property in order to create an income-producing rental suite.[2] Under the Canadian tax code, interest paid on money borrowed to earn income is tax deductible. Be on guard though—borrowing against your home is always a big risk and you should seek the help of a financial adviser who can guide you to the appropriate strategy.

## Mortgaged for Life

Committing to a mortgage for 25 or 30 years can seem daunting. It seems like a very long time. Your home and your neighbourhood will change. Your kids will have grown up, maybe with kids of their own, before you have finished paying. You, however, will be slimmer, taller and more distinguished-looking. More worldly, certainly.

Of course, you may choose to sell your home before your mortgage is fully amortized, as many people do. If you plan to trade up to a more expensive home, having more equity in your first mortgage will certainly help you in securing better terms for your new mortgage—and make that new home more affordable.

Whether you plan to stick it out until you are mortgage-free or trade up at some point, here are a few ways to minimize your interest, maximize your equity and help pay down that mortgage *faster*:

---

[2] Canada Customs and Revenue Agency (CCRA), "Income Tax Act: Interest Deductibility and Related Issues," CCRA Bulletin, October 31, 2003, http://www.cra-arc.gc.ca/E/pub/tp/it533/it533-e.pdf.

### 1. Make More Payments

As sure as the sun comes up every morning, your mortgage accrues interest each and every day. The quicker you can make payments, leaving as few days between each payment as possible, the less interest adds up. Here is an example: with a $280,000 mortgage amortized over 25 years, you will pay more than $126,000 in interest—making standard monthly payments. If you choose biweekly or weekly payments, you will reduce a bit of that interest because you will make 24 or 48 smaller payments per year, rather than the standard 12.

If you want to really amp up your payment power, consider accelerated payments. With an accelerated biweekly mortgage, you'll make 26 payments in a year, and 52 payments for the accelerated weekly. It doesn't sound like much, but sneaking in these few added payments can make a huge difference to the overall cost of your home. Using the example above, the biweekly accelerated option would reduce the length of your mortgage by *two years* compared to a standard monthly payment. More importantly, you would save $17,000 in interest payments. Surely you can think of something better to do with $17,000 than pay interest? If you switch to an accelerated weekly payment schedule, you will save even more. Each payment will be smaller than a monthly sum and easier to budget. We highly recommend increasing your payment frequency if you can swing it.

### 2. Top It Up When You Can

When you set out the terms of your mortgage, ask about the ability to make occasional lump-sum payments. Ideally, each year when you receive a tax refund, an annual bonus at work or a nice hefty birthday gift of cash from your granny, you can plop it right onto your mortgage.

Sticking with our example above, if you were to pay an extra $1,000 each year, you would pay off the mortgage *four years* sooner. Combine this with accelerated biweekly payments and you've just saved another $8,000 in interest costs. Yowsa!

When extra cash tempts you with its magical ability to buy stuff . . . just think about the oodles of disposable income you'll have when your mortgage is paid off. Short-term pain equals massive long-term gain.

### 3. Increase Those Dollars Down

Now that you're in the habit of paying your mortgage, you might think about bulking up on those payments. Over the years as you pay down your mortgage, you will probably manage to increase your income, giving you the means to pay off the loan faster. For example, imagine you got a raise worth $250 per month. Nice! Rather than spending it on baseball tickets, if you applied it to your mortgage, you would be mortgage-free *seven years* ahead of schedule *and* save $24,000 in interest. That could pay for a lot of ballpark hot dogs . . . and better seats to boot.

### 4. Lower Your Interest Rate

Interest rates have been blissfully low for years, but that doesn't mean you don't still have some negotiating room. Lenders are extremely competitive and you always have the opportunity to shop around, whether you are signing up for your first mortgage, trading in for a different one or renewing your old one. Even a few points off will save you a significant amount of cash. The difference between a 2.99 per cent rate and a 3.2 per cent rate adds up to about $6,000 in interest over the course of the mortgage. You will never know how low you can go unless you ask.

## Taking It Down a Notch

We love it when celebrities surprise us by being cooler and more down-to-earth than we ever expected. Case in point? Actor Tori Spelling and her (Canadian) husband, Dean McDermott. Despite growing up fabulously rich in Hollywood—in a nearly 57,000-square-foot "manor"(!)—and despite having four children, in 2011 Tori and Dean chose to "downsize" from a sprawling 6,700-square-foot Encino mansion to a 2,300-square-foot "cozy" Malibu home. Certainly, money wasn't a factor. Their decision was motivated by a desire to gather their growing family into closer quarters, so they would spend more time together. Beautiful, no?

As adviser and media personality (and Golden Girl Finance resident debt expert) Stephanie Holmes-Winton suggests, too many families get caught up in trading up—striving for ever bigger, more palatial and impressive homes. All too often, the extra room is unnecessary and the extra expense becomes a huge burden.

So why leave downsizing until your retirement years? Take a tip from Tori and Dean (and Stephanie!) and think about how taking your home down a notch might benefit not just your finances but your family too. After all, conspicuous consumption is *so* 1988.

Consider some of the benefits of downsizing:

- **More cash flow.** If you choose a less costly place, you will have more money to spend on experiences, such as travel and family vacations.
- **More time.** Less work and maintenance in yardwork and housecleaning.
- **More freedom.** Imagine living mortgage-free, maybe a whole decade sooner than would otherwise have been possible!
- **More family time.** The whole family hanging out together in one room? Watching the same movie, even? Yes, it has been done.

- **More convenience.** Moving to a smaller home means you might be able to afford a sweeter location, possibly with greater conveniences and closer to your favourite park, restaurant or other amenities.

- **Less stress.** Less house to heat, less stuff to fix, less property to manage.

- **Lower taxes.** With a smaller property, you will probably save a heap on property taxes too.

- **Less clutter.** Experience the lovely karma of letting go of all that stuff you never wanted in the first place that has been weighing you down for years.

- **Lead by example.** If you've told your kids that material possessions are not the most important things in life and reducing your environmental footprint is a good thing—show them how it's done!

---

**⚷━🔑 GOLDEN RULE: R MINUS 5**

If you are five years or less from your retirement and planning to sell your big, old, empty nest for a smaller, chicer, *pied-à-terre* befitting your new retirement status, the time is *now* to start the ball rolling. You want to score the best price you can for your home, since you will need the profit to see you through several years of green fees. Therefore, do not leave your real estate dreams to chance and last-minute market whims. Get a home appraisal done and check the comparables in your neighbourhood. You may need a few upgrades to get the price you want. Or, if the price you want is available to you now, why wait and risk uncertainty? We say grab the profit and ride off into that golden sunset.

As you know, you don't need the biggest, most expensive house on the block to feel happy and secure. Your neighbours living in that huge, fancy house likely feel *less secure* and more financially weighed down than anyone on the street. So skip the flash and focus on the kind of home that will keep you calm and not cash-poor. And remember: if you can't be with the home you love, honey, love the home you're with.

# 5

## Buy a New Car

*Car models don't change much year to year, but you can't put
a price on that new car smell. Ideally, you should be sporting a
new ride every two or three years and financing it (of course!)
for the longest term possible. If you do this for long enough, you
may end up owing more than your car is even worth. That's
okay—you'll look great doing it!*

Next time you stop at IKEA to stock up on tealights and Billy bookcases, check out what's parked in the parking lot. Probably a wide
mix of vehicles: cars, minivans and SUVs—maybe even a few luxury
sedans. Many of them will be newer models, most of them probably
no more than 10 years old. One thing is certain: none of those car
owners is as wealthy as IKEA founder Ingvar Kamprad. The 85-year-
old self-made multi-billionaire is the richest man in Europe and the
fifth-richest person in the world.[1] Yet, when Mr. Kamprad pulls up

---

[1] "Bloomberg Billionaires Index," Bloomberg (website), October 16, 2012, http://topics
.bloomberg.com/bloomberg-billionaires-index.

at his local IKEA in Sweden, he does so in his trusty 1993 Volvo 240 wagon. Quite possibly the cheapest car in the lot.

You probably shop at IKEA to be frugal. Yet when it comes to your choice of vehicle, if you were as frugal as Mr. Kamprad, you would have a much better shot at attaining even a fraction of his wealth.

## The Incredible Shrinking Asset

The first two major purchases you ever made (or will make) were very likely your home and your car. Not necessarily in that order.

Despite the wear and tear caused by kids, dogs and Canadian winters—a home is usually an appreciating asset. The land and location on which your house sits tend to increase in value over time. Buying low and selling high—the cardinal rule to follow in making any investment—is usually quite doable when it comes to a home.

The trouble with automobiles is that they rarely appreciate over time. With the exception of pristine vintage collector cars, your vehicle will almost certainly lose more of its value the longer you hold onto it and use it. If you buy a brand-new car, it will lose a huge chunk of value the moment you drive it off the dealer's lot. The more kilometres you drive, the less your car will be worth. Even if you manage to keep it in nearly perfect condition, the fact that newer, cooler versions of your car are introduced to the market every year makes your older model less and less valuable.

If you are not buying your car outright, you will make monthly payments on a vehicle whose value is dropping. Before long, the amount you owe on the car will be more than the car's resale value. If this were a house, we would call this "negative equity" (see Chapter 4). When it comes to vehicles, unfortunately, this is called "normal."

No way around it—cars are depreciating assets. Buying low and selling high is rarely possible when it comes to your car. (Unless of course, you're Warren Buffett, who, in 2007, auctioned off his used Lincoln Town Car on eBay for 10 times its value and gave the proceeds to Girls Inc., his charity.[2]) Therefore, it's best *not* to think of your car as an investment and instead think of it as what it is: a very big cost.

---

 **MUCH DEPRECIATED**

A car is a depreciating asset—the value will eventually drop to zero. Depreciation is an accounting term that defines exactly how much value your car loses each year. The depreciation cost is subtracted from your car's value, year after year—shrinking its worth. If you think of a balance sheet—with assets (the value of what you own) on one side and your liabilities (how much you owe) on the other—your goal with your car is to shrink your liability (what you owe) faster than your incredible shrinking asset (what the car is worth).

---

## You Call This a Luxury?

We hear your protests. For many busy working people and families living in rural communities, a car is no luxury: it is a practical necessity that enables you to get to work, to ferry around all the stuff you need for your household and to get the kids to daycare, school and soccer practice. However, let's put this in perspective. Consider all the families around the world—urban and rural— and all the lower-income, single parents who make do without a car. We are pretty spoiled in Canada. We have 620 vehicles for every 1,000 people, making us the fourteenth-highest car-owning

---

[2] "Going, Going, Gone—Warren Buffett Sells His Used Car," PR Newswire (website), n.d., http://www.prnewswire.com/news-releases/going-going-gone---warren-buffett-sells-his-used-car-to-the-learning-annex-president-for-10-times-its-value-57131247.html.

culture in the world.[3] Among middle-class Canadian households, it's rare to have fewer than *two* cars.[4] Fortunately, we are still slightly less "carred-up" than Brunei, Luxembourg, Monaco and the United States.

---

**⚿— GOLDEN RULE: LET SOMEONE ELSE PAY THE DEPRECIATION!**

Cars depreciate quickly within their first three years. After that, the rate of depreciation slows. Let someone else pay the brand-new car premium and instead find yourself a well-maintained, low-mileage, almost-new car that will hold its value for a longer time.

---

In the grand scheme of things, owning a car is a luxury, even if it has manual windows and you have to lock the doors with a key (gasp!). Yep, that cute Ford Focus is indeed a luxury. This is an important concept, because it will help you to keep things in perspective when considering how much you really need to splash out on that car.

So show a little more appreciation for your depreciating asset and let's figure out how to make it as cost-effective as possible, shall we? Essentially, there are three ways to pay: save up and pay cash, obtain financing and lease.

### 1. Save Up for It!

If you plan to buy your car without financing, we salute you! A vehicle—which is not an investment and depreciates from the moment you buy it—is an item that is best paid for out of money

---

[3] "List of Countries by Vehicles per Capita," Wikipedia (website), December 12, 2012, http://en.wikipedia.org/wiki/List_of_countries_by_vehicles_per_capita.

[4] The Canadian average in 2009 was 1.47 vehicles per household. Office of Energy Efficiency, Natural Resources Canada, "2009 Canadian Vehicle Survey," Natural Resources Canada (website), January 11, 2012, http://oee.rncan.gc.ca/publications/statistics/cvs09/chapter2.cfm?attr=0.

you have expressly saved up for the purpose. Paying for a vehicle outright means you will never be stuck owing more than it's actually worth. Best of all, you will pay zero interest fees, giving you a huge discount on the overall cost of your car, and the privilege of using that monthly cash of yours for much more rewarding things!

How much can you afford? Let's put it this way: How much can you save (without robbing from your retirement savings or emergency fund)?

## 2. Finance It

According to TD Canada Trust, the average price of a new car in Canada is more than $25,000.[5] While it would be awesome if everyone saved up that money before they went out and bought a car, many people instead turn to credit. With a car loan, you may pay for part of the purchase with a cash down payment, much as you would when buying a home with a mortgage. The larger your down payment, the less you will waste on interest fees. Banks and car dealerships both provide car loans. Typically, interest rates and associated fees at car dealerships are higher than bank loans—and all are highly negotiable—so make sure you do a comparison check before signing that contract.

Keep in mind that car dealers are motivated to help you squeeze any car into your budget! The more your eyes light up, the more creative they will be in helping you to figure out how to make the monthly payments and extend the length of your loan. Remember that just because it looks as if it could work on paper doesn't mean it will work in real life.

How much can you really afford? Your monthly payments must fit comfortably within your debt-to-income ratio (see Chapter 1).

---

[5] "Buying a Car in Canada," TD Canada Trust (website), n.d., http://www.tdcanadatrust.com/newtocanada/settling-in/buying-car.jsp.

The cost of servicing all your debt, including your car payments, mortgage and so on, should never be higher than 40 per cent of your gross income.

---

**⚿— GOLDEN RULE: FINANCING FINE POINTS**

If you choose to finance your car purchase, buy your car over a 36-month term and *no longer*. According to Golden Girl Finance's debt expert, Stephanie Holmes-Winton, if you can't afford the monthly payments based on a 36-month term, then you can't afford the car. (Sorry!) Go back to the lot or online listing and find something more economical that you can pay off in three years.

---

### 3. Lease It

The third way to own a car is to not really own it at all, that is, to lease rather than buy it. Leasing has become so popular these days, we sometimes wonder if it's not an addiction. And why is it that we never become addicted to things that are good for us? For many people, leasing is not a healthy choice.

What draws people in are the low, low monthly payments that leases offer. Well, who wouldn't want low payments, right? The trouble is, when you lease a car, you are not paying for the car, you are merely paying for the use of the car. Leasing is nothing more than long-term car rental with a lot of interest costs attached to it. At the end of your lease, you own nothing, not even that depreciated asset. But isn't that what you want anyway—the use of the car? Who cares who owns it? At the end of the lease, you just hand over the keys and start again with a new car. How cool is that?

The trouble with leasing is that you are locked into spending monthly sums that are filled with interest and finance charges.

We think there are better ways you could put your monthly cash flow to use, such as investing it and *earning* interest, rather than paying it.

There are three areas of cost you need to keep your eye on when leasing a car:

1. **The true interest rate and any fees.** Leasing companies were once notorious for padding interest rates and add-on fees. While this is less of a concern today, it is important to make sure you understand the full extent of what you will be paying for.

2. **The mileage you are permitted.** While you have the use of the car, you are allowed to drive a certain number of kilometres. If you drive past this point, you could suddenly be charged a whole lot more.

3. **The gap coverage.** Mind the gap! You will need insurance to cover the difference between what you owe on the lease and what your vehicle is worth. In case it is destroyed or stolen, you don't want to end up having to buy the car when it is worth less than the purchase price. If you take the amount you are considering spending on a lease and find a well-maintained used car—one whose first three years of depreciation are already paid for by someone else—you could probably get a much more reliable and valuable asset by spending the same amount. You will save money on interest if you pay for it outright and the car is yours to sell or trade in if you eventually choose to do so. Or you could be like Mr. Kamprad...choose a car for the long term and just keep on driving it!

From a tax perspective, many business owners prefer leasing, as it allows them to defer some taxes and to deduct a portion of their leasing cost. However, there are also tax breaks for car owners, so if you are considering leasing or buying a car for business purposes, make sure you compare the tax benefits specific to your situation.

---

**⚷ GOLDEN RULE: THE LEASE OF YOUR WORRIES**

According to debt expert Stephanie Holmes-Winton, leasing is suited *only* to those business owners with a legitimate ability to write off at least 50 per cent of the cost of the car. Even in this scenario, the following advice should be heeded: choose a car that you could afford to fully own within 36 months. Take the difference between your monthly lease payment and the would-be monthly loan payment and put that extra cash into a savings account—perhaps for the purchase of your next car or even a family holiday!

---

## Buying It Is One Thing...Keeping It Is Another

According to the Canada Mortgage and Housing Corporation (CMHC), the average cost of owning and operating a vehicle in Canada is more than $9,000 annually.[6] That works out to almost $25 a day, which may be worthwhile if you're doing a long commute and a lot of driving. However, if your car is parked for 20 to 22 hours of the day, you might want to think about spending less on that all-important car and freeing up some of that money to spend on more *relevant* things.

Generally speaking, car costs fall into two categories: ownership and operation.

---

[6] "Greenhouse Gas Emissions from Urban Travel," CMHC and Natural Resources Canada, 2000, http://www.cmhc-schl.gc.ca/en/inpr/su/sucopl/grgaem/upload/Green-Gas-Emissions_E.pdf.

*Ownership Costs*

These fall into your initial outlay, as addressed above. Most people choose a car based on the monthly payments and then find themselves cash-poor when they realize the total purchase price. Don't let this be you! Your overall purchase price will include:

- Price of your car ÷ monthly payments
- Taxes
- Insurance
- Licence and registration

Ownership means so much more than buying. Ownership is a commitment to costs that just keep on costing, every year. The Canadian Automobile Association (CAA) came up with the information shown in Table 5.1 to give you an idea of average annual car ownership costs. For a full explanation of the factors used in this calculation, visit their site at www.caa.ca and check out "Driving Costs."[7]

**Table 5.1:** Average annual car ownership costs

|  | Honda Civic LX (4 cylinder) | Toyota Camry LE (4 cylinder) | Chevrolet Equinox LT |
|---|---|---|---|
| Insurance | $2,467.44 | $2,667.00 | $2,773.68 |
| Licence and registration | $ 124.00 | $ 124.00 | $ 124.00 |
| Depreciation | $3,024.00 | $3,633.48 | $4,608.00 |
| Financing/loan | $ 824.28 | $1,025.52 | $1,286.64 |
| Annual total | $6,439.72 | $7,450.00 | $8,792.32 |
| Cost per day* | $ 17.64 | $ 20.41 | $ 24.09 |

* All cars 2012 model year; cost per day excludes operating costs.

[7] CAA, *Driving Costs*, 2012 edition (Ottawa: Canadian Automobile Association), n.d., http://caa.ca/docs/eng/CAA_Driving_Costs_English.pdf.

Keep in mind, these are just the costs of owning the car. We'll talk about the added cost of upkeep next.

### Operating Costs

Once you've taken care of the fixed costs of owning the car, you still need to deal with the not-so-little matter of keeping it working. Operating costs are definitely a function of use: the more you use the car, the higher your operating costs will be. However, as we pointed out earlier, if you're not getting enough use out of your car to justify the amount it costs, perhaps you should consider a different strategy, such as car sharing, which we will look at later in this chapter.

Operating costs must be manageable within your monthly cash flow, in other words, you need to be able to cover them with what's left over after all your monthly debts and obligations are paid. Operating costs include:

- Fuel (and the price of gas just keeps going up!)
- Maintenance (including winter tires, summer tires, afternoon tires, etc.)
- Servicing and repairs (the fancier the car, the costlier the repairs)
- Parking (in some cities, equivalent to the price of rent for a studio apartment)

The CAA has put together handy reference guides to show what the average car owner can expect to spend (see tables 5.2 to 5.4). We've included them here, because, well, it's always fun to be a bit of a voyeur on what other people spend, isn't it? These examples are just for illustration purposes: actual costs will vary depending on your own arrangements

**Table 5.2:** 2012 Honda Civic LX (4 cylinder) annual driving costs

| Km driven per year | Operating costs | Ownership costs | Total cost | Cost per km |
|---|---|---|---|---|
| 12,000 | $1,548.00 | $6,175.72 | $7,723.72 | $0.64 |
| 16,000 | $2,064.00 | $6,439.72 | $8,503.72 | $0.53 |
| 18,000 | $2,322.00 | $6,439.72 | $8,761.72 | $0.49 |
| 24,000 | $3,096.00 | $6,691.72 | $9,787.72 | $0.41 |
| 32,000 | $4,128.00 | $7,171.72 | $11,299.72 | $0.35 |

**Table 5.3:** 2012 Toyota Camry LE (4 cylinder) annual driving costs

| Km driven per year | Operating costs | Ownership costs | Total cost | Cost per km |
|---|---|---|---|---|
| 12,000 | $2,001.60 | $7,140.52 | $9,142.12 | $0.76 |
| 16,000 | $2,668.80 | $7,450.00 | $10,118.80 | $0.63 |
| 18,000 | $3,002.40 | $7,450.00 | $10,452.40 | $0.58 |
| 24,000 | $4,003.20 | $7,752.52 | $11,755.72 | $0.49 |
| 32,000 | $5,337.60 | $8,316.52 | $13,654.12 | $0.43 |

**Table 5.4:** 2012 Chevrolet Equinox LT annual driving costs

| Km driven per year | Operating costs | Ownership costs | Total cost | Cost per km |
|---|---|---|---|---|
| 12,000 | $1,972.80 | $8,492.32 | $10,465.12 | $0.87 |
| 16,000 | $2,630.40 | $8,792.32 | $11,422.72 | $0.71 |
| 18,000 | $2,959.20 | $8,792.32 | $11,751.52 | $0.65 |
| 24,000 | $3,945.60 | $9,068.32 | $13,013.92 | $0.54 |
| 32,000 | $5,260.80 | $9,584.32 | $14,845.12 | $0.46 |

and where you live. For a full explanation of these costs, visit www.caa.ca and check out "Driving Costs."

## Car Buying Checklist

If, after all, you decide you must own a car, here are a few things to keep in mind:

- ✓ **Arrange your financing before you go car-hunting.** Find out what your bank can do for you first—you'll know what you can truly afford and you will be in a better bargaining position when the dealership offers you a loan.

- ✓ **Know what the car is objectively worth.** If you're buying a used car, do your research before agreeing to a price. Check comparables online and find out the "black book" depreciated value for the make and model you are hoping to score. Here is a site to help get you started: http://www.canadianblackbook .com/black-book-values.

- ✓ **Keep your trade-in a secret until you have a firm price on the car.** If they ask, be non-committal. Dealers will sometimes inflate the price if they know there will be a request for a discount with a trade-in.

- ✓ **Remember that everything is negotiable,** especially if you're paying in cash.

- ✓ **Watch out for the extras!** Once you've said yes, that's when all the fun and costly extra features become available. It's like all those handy items conveniently placed around the cash register that entice you once your wallet is out. Do not impulse-buy when it comes to your car. Know what features you're willing to pay for and what you can live without *before* you sit down to sign the agreement.

## What If It's Too Late?

Oh no! If only you had read this book *before* you signed up for seven years of car payments! Now you have the most beautiful car you have ever owned, fully loaded with the climate-control package and the multimedia option, and it looks fabulous sitting in your driveway. Sadly, you can't drive it because your monthly payments are so high you can't afford to fill it with gas. Once you have signed, sealed and driven a car off into the sunset, it can be awfully difficult to go back to the dealer with your depreciated set of wheels and try to change the terms. All is not lost. Depending on your payment schedule and the type of vehicle, you may just be able to find a way to trade down. If your expensive car is stressing you out, here are a few options from Stephanie Holmes-Winton worth trying:

1. **Return to the dealer.** Okay, you may have your tail between your legs, but looking humble usually helps. It may be tricky or even impossible to convince a dealer to let you swap your car for a less costly one, but it's not unprecedented and definitely worth a try. If the good news is that the dealer will let you trade down, be prepared for the bad news. There is a pretty good chance that the value of your car has dropped since you bought it—and it may even be worth less than what you still owe. For example, suppose you bought the car at $35,000 and you still owe $25,000. The car has depreciated, however, and is now worth only $20,000. Don't think the dealer will forget about that $5,000. Even if you trade down to a cheaper car, that $5,000 will get tacked on to its purchase price.

2. **Sell the car.** In the example above, the price of the new, "cheaper" car—the one you trade down for—could end up being around the same as, or more than, the depreciated value of the car you originally bought. In this case, you might be better off selling the car for its current value and paying off your loan. You will need to check the rules in your loan

agreement, however. If the loan is attached to the value of the car, then you might not be able to sell it out from under the loan.

3. **Get back in the market.** Dealers are very competitive and there is a chance that another dealer would be willing to help you out in the interest of securing a new loan for themselves. Shop around and visit other car dealers in your area: you very well might be able to get a better trade and the reduced payments you need.

4. **Sell your contract.** Take comfort in knowing that you are not the first person in the position of wanting to trade down. There are plenty of online businesses that provide a marketplace for people looking to trade cars or contracts, and you just might find someone who is willing to assume the terms of your loan and take the car off your hands. Try www .LeaseBusters.com, www.Craigslist.ca, www.Kijiji.ca or www.eBay.ca/Motors as a start.

## Burning Man, Anyone?

Find yourself burning through gas at an alarming rate? Here are a few tips to keep your fuel costs down and your vehicle running a little more smoothly. Hey, whatever it takes to keep those operating costs down, right?

- **Shop competitively.** No two gas stations charge alike and you may be paying a few cents' premium just because you prefer the energy drink selection across the street.

- **Power down.** Buying a car with a smaller engine may not seem manly but it will make you wealthier—and doesn't money equal power? Six cylinders use up more gas than four and, unless you're doing some track time on the side, all that engine will probably be wasted on trips to the grocery store.

- **Make appropriate choices.** Your car will run more efficiently if you use the type of gas it was made to use. Check the owner's manual and discover what really makes your car tick.

- **Pump it up.** It takes a car more effort to move properly if the tires are low on air. Make sure they are pumped up. (They often sag after temperature changes.)

- **Look under the hood.** The CAA says that engine problems can increase the amount of gas you use by up to 50 per cent. Make sure your transmission, steering, brakes and air filters are all checked out and working properly.

- **Lighten up.** The more stuff you stow in your car, the heavier it is, and the heavier it is, the more fuel it burns. Remove unneeded roof racks, spare tires and sports gear. Your car is not a garage.

- **Go beyond.** Short trips keep the engine from performing at its peak operating level, so combine your errands and make fewer trips that last longer. Short trips? Walk!

- **Slow down.** It's not us, it's the CAA that says so. Reducing your speed from 120 km/h to 100 km/h can reduce your fuel usage by as much as 20 per cent.

---

**⚷ GOLDEN RULE: WHY DRIVE WHEN YOU CAN WALK?**

Need to wean your family off its car addiction? After-dinner family strolls are a good start. Save the drive for essential trips and get your family riding bikes and walking. Grouchy dispositions will magically improve when the opportunity for backseat arguments is removed.

## Carless Alternatives

Alright, we have talked about buying, financing and leasing cars. But what if your best and cheapest car option is no car at all? After all, if your car is costing you $9,000 a year to own and operate (or $25 a day), and you only use it for an hour or two each day, then why bother owning it at all?

Of course you know all about public transportation and car pooling and biking to work. These are the traditional socks-and-Birkenstocks alternatives to car ownership.

Renting cars has always been a great option for weekend drivers—those people who only need a car to drive their little old grandmother to church on Sundays, or to drive to IKEA to load up on more Billy bookcases. The old-style car-rental agencies, with their bureaucracy, paperwork and inconvenient airport locations, have happily been replaced by a new model that is cheap and peppy, just the way we like it. We're talking, of course, about car-sharing services.

With a car-sharing service, you sign up as a member and receive a keycard or a key to a lockbox. Cars are parked in designated parking lots all over town, and when you need one for an hour or a day, you go online and book the vehicle you want. When you're done with the car, you drop it off in the lot and move on with your life. Here in Canada, some of the bigger national brands include www.Zipcar .ca and www.Car2Go.com, but there are also local car-sharing companies popping up in cities and towns all over the country.

## The Low-Car Diet

In 2009, Zipcar enlisted 250 people from 13 cities across the United States. All of these people were not only car owners but self-confessed "car addicts." In a challenge called the Low-Car Diet, Zipcar convinced the participants to surrender their car keys for one month.

For an entire month, they could not use their cars at all. They had to rely on walking, biking, taking public transportation or plain old bumming a ride from their pals. Each participant was given a Zipcar membership—but it was only to be used when *absolutely* necessary.

As you might expect, the results demonstrated a few healthy changes:

- 132 per cent increase in miles biked
- 93 per cent increase in miles walked
- 66 per cent decrease in miles driven

While 413 pounds (187 kilograms) were lost, the really astonishing bit was that after the month was up, rather than racing back to their cars, 100 people out of the 250 decided they did not want their keys back. A full 61 per cent said that from then on, they would be car-free.

It is hard to imagine giving up your car, but the Low-Car Diet proves it is possible. Since 2009, people in other cities, including Toronto and Vancouver, have been trying to go carless. If you can't fathom the idea, try baby steps: use your car only on weekdays and enjoy car-free weekends. Or try the reverse and use your car only on weekends. Breaking free of your car addiction is healthy, liberating and inspiring!

---

 **THANKS, BIKERS!**

Reducing the number of vehicles on the road not only makes our air cleaner, it reduces the stress on our cities' infrastructure and utilities. In Vancouver, 2,700 people bike into downtown during morning rush hour. That is the equivalent of 50 full transit buses.[8]

---

[8] Zipcar, http://ir.zipcar.com/releasedetail.cfm?ReleaseID=608343.

## A Cultural Shift

Rachel Botsman is an expert on how people collaborate and the ways in which our society is changing. When she saw the first results of Zipcar's Low-Car Diet, she declared that these people simply lost the urge to own. Ms. Botsman feels this is consistent with a larger collective movement happening in our society, where access is valued over ownership.[9] Think about that for a moment: Do you want the DVD or do you want to watch the movie? Do you want the CD or just want to listen to the music whenever you want? Do you want the book or the story?

When it comes to cars, this cultural shift explains both the sustained popularity in automobile leasing and the new growth in car-sharing services. As we mentioned earlier, many people aren't concerned about owning a car, they just want access to it.

Certainly we invest our vehicles with more personal significance than a CD. We also use our vehicles repeatedly, much more often than a DVD. But there is potential for change. We've come a long way from the 1980s when the ownership of a posh car (or several!) was viewed as a sign of success. Nowadays, it's becoming a sign of greed.

## You Are Not What You Drive

To misquote Sigmund Freud, sometimes a car is just a car. We all know how lovely it is to enjoy a smooth ride in a fancy set of wheels now and then. Ultimately, however, your car is just transportation— a means of getting you to your destination. Getting caught up in a status competition when it comes to cars almost always leads to bad financial decisions, not to mention self-esteem issues.

---

[9] Rachel Botsman, "The Case for Collaborative Consumption," TED Conversations, YouTube video, accessed December 16, 2012, http://www.ted.com/talks/rachel_botsman_the_case_for_collaborative_consumption.html.

If you rely on your car to make a statement about who you are, keep in mind that not everyone will read that message in the same way. We guarantee that some people will interpret what your car says about you in a way you might not like.

There will always be people who choose cars to make themselves look wealthier and more prosperous than they are. You, smarty-pants, will be the wiser one who chooses a car that won't impair your ability to build wealth. Like Ingvar Kamprad, don't look rich—be rich.

# 6

## Take a Vacation

*Pull out your credit card and go somewhere nice. There's nothing better than getting away from it all, and you totally deserve it! After all, you want to be able to brag about this for years to come. (Plus, you look great with a tan . . .)*

Ahhh, vacation. Just the word is enough to make you sigh deeply, slow down your heart rate and put a dreamy smile on your face.

The trouble is finding that rare confluence of time and money that makes taking a vacation possible. It seems that when work is busy and you're earning great money, you have no ability to take time off and break away for a holiday. When work slows down or you're between jobs, the last thing you want to do is blow your limited supply of cash on a vacation. (Come to think of it, you are looking a little pale . . .)

And yet, every now and then the stars do align and you figure out a way to take a break. Maybe it's just a little weekend getaway or maybe it's a well-deserved sojourn in a far-flung destination. Either way, one thing we can assure you is that vacation spending tends to have an inverse relationship with vacation planning. So take the time to plan, to research and to save up your cash, and you are far more likely to get much more mileage out of those vacation dollars. In this chapter, we will look at some of the ways you can do just that.

---

**🔑 GOLDEN RULE: SAVING FOR A SUNNY DAY**

You want to relax, don't you? When you return from a holiday, the tan fades too quickly, you're back at work and it's like you never left. You will feel even more deflated upon your return if you have to spend the next several months paying off a massive credit card bill. How much more lovely to save up first and then relax on your vacation, knowing your pina coladas are already paid for? Once you return home and the realities of everyday life set in, you are free to start planning and saving for your next adventure.

---

## Credit Cards: Friend or Foe?

When it comes to travelling on vacation, credit cards can be your best friend or your worst enemy. It's all in the way you use them. First, the ways in which plastic can be your friend:

- Many credit cards offer travel-specific benefits such as trip insurance or points that can be used for booking flights or hotel rooms.

- There is a certain security in using your credit card on holiday—your credit card company will have your back if there are strange charges or problems with purchases or bookings. Make sure to call and give them a heads-up on your travel plans, however, or you may find yourself locked out when you're innocently trying to buy a tribal mask from a cute tiki hut in Bali.

- The foreign exchange conversion rates on purchases you make with your credit card are often better than what you can get exchanging cash. Some cards tack on an extra currency conversion fee of 1–3 per cent, but many credit cards oriented to the international traveller do not, so check before you spree.

- Credit cards are light, lean and easy to cancel if they get lost or stolen. Fat stacks of cash, on the other hand, are vulnerable: when they're gone, they're gone.

- If you have cashback or point-collecting features on your credit card, putting all your big-ticket vacation expenditures on your credit card will reap you an extra bonus to enjoy post-holiday. (Just make sure you pay off the balance before any interest is due.)

And then there are the traits that make credit cards fearsome travel companions:

- Unlike using cash, you may find it tougher to stick to a budget when you're blindly putting everything on a credit card. Be diligent about keeping your receipts and doing a once-a-day tally in order to keep your spending somewhat tethered to reality.

- Loading up your credit card with holiday expenses is advisable only if you've already saved up the cash to pay off the balance. You don't want the memories of your relaxing, wonderful vacation to be tainted by 18.5 per cent interest-rate charges.

**THE MONEY CHANGERS**

When it comes to exchanging your bucks for a foreign currency, most travellers don't know which way to turn. You step up to the counter and hope for the best. Sound familiar? Fear not. Here are your options—from our top recommendation to our least favourite:

- **Credit cards.** Using your credit card to pay for purchases will most often give you the best exchange rate. A 2011 study[1] confirmed that Visa and MasterCard provided the best rates, particularly on credit cards that did not add on any currency conversion (a.k.a. international) fees.

- **ATM/bank exchanges.** At some point, you will need cash. Withdrawing from the ATM is your best bet, though some banks charge higher fees to non-customers. If you can find a home bank ATM, so much the better. Also, try to make as few withdrawals as possible. The study found that banks' exchange rates resulted in up to an 8 per cent higher cost than that charged on a credit card with no international exchange fee. However, each bank is different: if your credit card does charge an international fee, the rates may be comparable.

- **Currency exchange counters.** Yes, they are oh-so-conveniently located in airport lounges, but you pay a premium for that convenience. The study found that the cost of exchange at these companies can be up to 16.2 per cent higher than that charged on a credit card with no international exchange fee.

## Just Say No to Dynamic Currency Conversion

You're strolling through a lovely shop in Cabo San Lucas, and you decide to purchase a beautiful silver bracelet as a gift for a

---

[1] "Currency Exchange Study," CardHub (website), June 11, 2012, http://education.cardhub.com/currency-exchange-study.

special someone. You hand over your credit card and before the cashier swipes it, she kindly asks if you'd prefer the transaction to be charged in Canadian dollars. If you're using a hand-held device, the option may be presented to you on the screen. Of course, you think, this makes it so much easier to budget and account for later.

*No, no, no!* This service is called "dynamic currency conversion," or sometimes "cardholder preferred currency," and is offered by merchants in order to make a little extra on the transaction. You will be charged the cost of the bracelet based on whatever the merchant chooses as the prevailing exchange rate, *plus* a 2–3 per cent markup, *plus* a 2–3 per cent extra fee. Instead, choose to be billed in the local currency: your credit card will convert the currency (usually at a better rate than the merchant offers) plus a transaction fee, but, overall, it will be less costly for you.

---

 **MEMORIES OF INTEREST**

Suppose you splash out and take a fabulous two-week holiday in the Caribbean. You come home and a few weeks later, there it is. Your credit card statement. You tentatively tear open the envelope and look through squinted eyes at the total damage. Yikes: $8,000! But hold on, the minimum payment is only $240—that's doable, right? Wrong. If you pay only the minimum amount and your credit card company charges you 18.9 per cent interest, you will be paying for that two-week holiday for *the next four years*. You will also pay an extra $3,461 in interest over that time, increasing the total cost of your trip to $11,461. Instead, pay off the $8,000 right away with the cash you prudently saved in advance. Now you are free to start saving and planning for your next holiday. (That's a little more refreshing, isn't it?)

## How to Take an Interest-Rate Vacation

If you pay attention to your credit card payment cycle, you can avoid paying interest charges and use your credit card the way it should be used: as an interest-free loan.

First there is the time that elapses between the moment you make your purchase and the end of the billing period. No interest is charged within this window. Then there is the grace period between the statement date (the date printed on the statement, *not* the date you physically receive it) and the payment-due date. If you can time your purchases and payments to align with your credit card cycle, you can take a vacation not just from work but from interest payments as well!

## Safe Travels: Your Guide to Travel Insurance

So, you've plunked down the cash on the airline tickets, reserved the hotels, booked the car, and bitten the bullet on the taxes. The last thing a traveller wants is one more expense. And yet there it is—just as you hand over your credit card—would you like insurance with that? Well, do you? If you're like many people, you have only a vague idea of what you are covered for and what extra insurance you ought to purchase for your holiday. Your travel agent, online booking site, airline, car rental agency and even your bank will all try to sell you extra insurance.

So what are the things you need to insure against and where's the best place to get value for your dollar? Here are eight tips to keep you covered:

1. **Trip cancellation insurance.** If you have to cancel that all-inclusive at the last minute, trip cancellation insurance can save you a bundle. Flights alone, however, sometimes come with built-in insurance. **TIP:** Check the restrictions on your

ticket carefully: the change fee and potential fare increase might be less than the cost of cancellation insurance.

2. **Trip delay insurance.** You arrive at the airport only to find that your flight has been delayed, re-routed or cancelled. This can mean a day spent eating airport food or even a night at the airport hotel. Your airline may or may not cover these costs for you. **TIP:** Check with your credit card company and your frequent flyer card to see if they offer extra help, such as covering hotel costs and help in booking new flights, in these circumstances.

3. **Lost baggage insurance.** Most airlines offer a per diem to help tide you over until your bags show up, but these are quite small and it's unlikely you can duplicate all your wardrobe and cosmetic needs on $25 or $50. If the airline fully loses your bags, it will reimburse you, but it takes time and the amount they offer may seem paltry compared to what you've lost. **TIP:** Some gold, platinum or travel-point credit cards offer immediate reimbursement on lost luggage or a higher per diem than the airlines.

4. **Loss and theft insurance.** If you are worried about your video camera being stolen, check with your home insurance policy, which may offer some compensation for loss (though the deductible might be high). If you purchased the camera recently, you may have the option of seeking replacement through your credit card or debit card purchase insurance. **TIP:** Be sure to ask your insurance provider about specific items you are concerned about. Might be best to leave the diamond necklace at home.

5. **Medical insurance.** Heaven forbid you fall ill or have a medical emergency while you're travelling, but if you do, the last thing you're going to want to worry about is how to pay for it.

Check your employer benefits as well as your credit cards to see what they cover when you travel before you buy extra insurance through your travel agency, bank or insurance company. Some policies require you to pay upfront and then reimburse you later, while other policies cover the costs for you on the spot. Some policies cover emergency treatment only and not hospital stays, while some policies even cover the cost of airlifting you home from another country. These are important distinctions and the level of comprehensiveness is reflected in the cost. **TIP:** Read the fine print and carry the insurer's toll-free emergency number with you at all times.

6. **Car rental insurance.** The car rental company will be eager to sell you their top package. Check with your credit card company, which may cover you for theft or any damage that happens to the car while you've rented it. Read the rules and limitations carefully. When it comes to liability coverage in case someone gets hurt or you damage someone else's property with the car, it is advisable to be covered for a high amount, on the theory that if something goes wrong, it tends to go really, really wrong. If you already own a car, your auto-insurance policy may include car rentals, and any auto association you belong to may also include liability insurance. **TIP:** Top-up liability insurance policies offered by car rental companies often are not as good value as those you can buy through provincial government insurance such as ICBC, SGI or any of the major banks and private insurance companies.

7. **Liability insurance.** Accidents happen. If you accidentally set the beach hut on fire or the roof flies off your house back at home and crashes onto your neighbours' car, you will be thankful for general liability coverage. This is the same kind of insurance you get to cover accidents with a car rental; it

just extends to all other unfortunate circumstances. **TIP:** This is usually covered within any all-inclusive travel insurance, but read the fine print.

8. **All-inclusive travel insurance.** If you want the security of being covered for every potential outcome, talk to a travel agency, bank or insurance company. While there may be an extra commission attached to the policy, the advantage here is that you can speak with an adviser to help you sort out exactly what coverage you get for your money. **TIP:** These providers also offer multi-trip insurance, which can be handy and economical if you have several trips coming up over the course of the year.

The whole point of taking a holiday is to let your cares slip away, relax with loved ones and enjoy your surroundings. When it comes to travel insurance, if you do it right, any hassle and expense is handled upfront before you go away. Ideally, this will allow you to chill out even more, knowing that if something goes awry, you've got it covered. Happy travels!

## Hotels Are *So* 2008

Staying in a wonderful hotel can be a trip unto itself. When you're on a budget, however, high room rates, tipping and extra fees for every little thing can take all the joy out of an otherwise relaxing stay. If only you had a cousin with a swish pad you could rent for a fraction of the hotel cost!. You could live like a local, save cash and enjoy a more authentic experience of life in your holiday destination.

Well, who needs cousins anymore? There is a whole world out there of people willing to rent out or swap their houses, condos and cottages to someone just like you. Let's consider a few options:

## Private Rentals

"Peer-to-peer accommodation services," as the financiers like to call them, are turning what was once a slightly nerve-wracking, edgy alternative to hotel stays into a slick, professional and highly reputable business. In addition to finding a unique and amazing place to spend your vacation, you might consider using a service to rent out your own place while you're away, giving you some extra cash to pay for your holiday. Make your house earn its keep for once!

Many sites come fully-loaded with insurance policies, but for those that don't, make sure you make your own arrangements to cover your butt while travelling or while renting out.

Here are a few sites to get you thinking:

- www.AirBnb.com
- www.HomeAway.com
- www.VRBO.com
- www.OwnersDirect.co.uk
- www.OneFineStay.com
- www.HouseTrip.com

## Home-Swapping

In the 2006 film *The Holiday*, Cameron Diaz and Kate Winslet play two single women who switch homes, get a taste for one another's way of life and, of course, find romance and live happily ever after. They used the real-life home-swapping site www.HomeExchange .com to trade a posh Los Angeles pad with a cozy English cottage.

The way it works is like this: you search the listings, find a place you like, contact the owners, get to know them a little online and see if there's an interest in swapping homes as a low-cost way to go. Think of it as Internet dating, except with your house.

Incidentally, home-swapping is not just for singles. Think of it as a great big online key party—without the creepy 1970s implications! Check out these sites as possibilities; some offer the option of renting if swapping isn't your thing:

- www.HomeExchange.com
- www.HomeLink.org
- www.SabbaticalHomes.com
- www.Intervac.ca
- www.CasaSwap.com

## Time-Shares

They still do this? Of course! If you haven't taken the bait of a free day at a spa or a night at that cool hotel with the waterslides for the kids, all in exchange for a "quick, half-hour seminar" that ends up costing you an entire day and having to endure a very high-pressure sales pitch—well, you just haven't lived.

When you buy a time-share, you buy access to a holiday home— usually one week per year. You are essentially buying 1/52nd of a property. Time-share properties can be condominiums, houseboats, ski chalets, cottages or even dude ranches. The attraction of time-shares is that they allow you to have all of the conveniences of a condominium without the expense, upkeep or responsibility of buying and maintaining an entire property. Time-shares have evolved to include properties at all-inclusive resorts, hotel suites and whole portfolios of properties that allow you to register your week and trade it for use at other properties. As long as you have the flexibility to match your vacation schedule with the availability of the property, you will be good to go.

Many people love the idea of having a prepaid vacation: they see it as a way to make sure they take their allotted holiday time.

It's all too easy to let a year slip by without taking your two weeks. Indeed, Canadians collectively forego 32 million vacation days every year—we are *so* hardworking![2] On the downside, time-shares often come loaded with a lot of heavy marketing expenses, giving them a bad rep. However, if you do your research, a time-share purchased *in the secondary market* can be a very savvy investment.

A secondary market is an online site where people sell their time-shares. These are usually at a considerable discount to the developer's original prices. Think of it as buying a used car instead of a brand new car: there's quite a bit of depreciation the moment it comes off the lot.

However, as with buying a used car, you must do your research and be very careful about the quality and condition of what you are buying. Here are a few sites where you can find out more information about time-share secondary markets:

- www.TUG2.net (Time-share Users Group)
- www.eBay.com
- www.SellMyTimeshareNow.com
- www.TimeshareCanada.com

Time-share expert and author Joy Wood recommends that you ask the following tough questions before making a commitment on the secondary market:

✓ How popular is the destination? If it's very popular, it will also be more "liquid," meaning that, in the event you don't use it, it will be easier to trade or resell.

---

[2] Alison Ramsey, "Vacation Trends in the Workplace," Readers' Digest (website), n.d., http://www.readersdigest.ca/travel/tips/vacation-trends-workplace.

✓ How popular is the resort company? If the company itself has a great brand and a reputation for quality, your time-share will be more valuable if you wish to trade.

✓ Can you buy a week during a certain season or during special events? If the resort tends to fill up during certain times of the year, buying a week at that time will ensure you can sell your week if you need to.

✓ Are you purchasing a limited time-share or a deeded week? This determines whether you have access to the time-share for a set (limited) number of years, as opposed to the kind (deeded) that can be passed on to your kids.

✓ Check out the "reserve"—with a time-share, as with any condominium, you need to know if funds have been set aside in reserve for any major repairs the property requires. If there is no reserve, you could be in for a costly surprise.

✓ Is there a budget and plan for furniture replacement and general upkeep and refurbishment of the property over the long term?

✓ Are you buying a floating week or a fixed week? Are you able to commit to a fixed vacation each year or do you need greater flexibility? If your fixed week is during a popular time of the year, you will have greater trading power. A low-season time-share, however, can make for a more leisurely vacation.

✓ What are the maintenance fees and how much have they gone up over the last five years? This can give you an indication of how much the time-share will cost you in the future.

✓ Does the property have the amenities you need? Features such as a full kitchen and outdoor pool give you the opportunity to eat in and enjoy more relaxed family time.

**SUMMER DREAMS**

While a warmer climate might be appealing during our cold Canadian winter, summertime remains the favourite time of year for Canadians to take vacations. According to a CIBC survey, 55 per cent of Canadians plan a summer vacation, with the average person planning to spend $1,728 on their holiday. Three-quarters plan their trips within Canada (and why not? We have gorgeous summers!), while 24 per cent visit the United States and 9 per cent plan to travel outside North America.[3]

## Staycation, Anyone?

As a wisecracking (but wise) anonymous author once said, "The alternative to taking a vacation is to stay home and tip every third person you see." While that doesn't sound like much fun, staying home for a vacation can be truly rejuvenating, if you do it right.

Maybe you have a lifelong plan to go on an African safari or you dream of visiting Paris in the spring. It might take you a year or two to set aside the necessary funds. While you save up for that big adventure, you don't have to settle for no adventure at all. Enter the staycation! Discover the pleasure to be found on your own home turf. Many hotels offer great last-minute weekend deals, so you can feel like you're away from home even if you're just a few miles away. Check out the private home-rental sites and see what it's like to live in a totally different neighbourhood for a few days. Try out that restaurant you've been meaning to get to. Go to a concert. Visit local

---

[3] CIBC, "School's Out—Canadians Spending $1,700 on Average for Vacations This Summer," Press Release, Canada News Wire (website), June 29, 2012, http://www.newswire.ca/en/story/1001475/cibc-poll-school-s-out-canadians-spending-1-700-on-average-for-vacations-this-summer.

parks, attractions and festivals you have never bothered to frequent before. You might be impressed by what other tourists already know about your city! The best part: no airport lineups, currency exchange or immunizations required.

## Last-Minute Clubs

If you want to head further afield, last-minute clubs and booking sites can offer amazing deals on flights, hotels and vacation packages. If you have the flexibility—and the adventurous spirit—to leave on a few days' or few weeks' notice and are open to a variety of destinations, you will have the opportunity to choose from among some great bargains.

Many websites offer these last-minute deals to members who sign up for weekly newsletters or email alerts. Set your budget and a general timeline and watch for the deal that meets your criteria. Some examples include Air Canada's Wednesday "websaver" deals, www.SellOffVacations.com and the aptly named www.LastMinuteClub.com. Holiday package providers also feature last-minute deals on their websites, such as Air Canada Vacations' Last Minute Deals, www.Sunwing.ca and Transat Holidays.

## All-Inclusive: Yay or Nay?

Generally speaking, all-inclusives are a great way to spend a lot less than you would by putting together your own custom holiday experience. Booking flights and hotels and paying for separate meals will almost always add up to more than the all-inclusive packaged holiday rates. Still, the all-inclusives are not for everyone: many people feel constrained by eating at the same resort every day and want to get out and experience more of what the local community has to offer. However, for those looking for a restful experience, where they don't have to plan, think or pull out their wallet, all-inclusives can be the perfect choice.

## Cheap and Cheerful

Cheaper options always make us more cheerful. Here are a few tips for cheaper, more cheerful travelling experiences:

- **Fly mid-week.** According to a study conducted by www .FareCompare.com, Wednesday is the cheapest day to fly. If you're booking a week off work, who says it can't be from Wednesday to Wednesday? If you can get a statutory holiday in there, it's even more advantageous.

- **Take advantage of shoulder seasons.** Every destination has its low- and high-season rates. If you can avoid travelling when everyone else does, you can save a lot of money on the same holiday. Late fall and spring (outside of Easter and spring break) are often referred to as the "shoulder seasons," when flights and hotel rates are low. Check the destination you plan to visit: you don't want to save money just to end up in the middle of monsoon season!

- **Eat in.** If there's one thing that will eat up your travel budget fast, it's food. For many people, dining out and trying local food are essential to vacation fun, but eating in restaurants three times a day will slim your wallet while padding your waistline. Take a local rather than a tourist approach to eating: skip the costly hotel breakfast and stock your room with snacks and a few basics from a local grocery store. Save your dining splurges for one special meal a day—either lunch or dinner—and eat inexpensive takeout for other meals. If you stay somewhere with a kitchen, you can balance rich restaurant meals with a few simple home-cooked dinners.

- **Pack light.** Wouldn't it be fun to go on a holiday with nothing but a swimsuit and a credit card? It would certainly save you money on checked-luggage fees—some airlines now charge up to $25 a bag. For the sake of your sanity as well as your budget, it is well worth trying to avoid checking bags or paying over-weight baggage fees. Focus your wardrobe on a few essentials you love to wear at home, plus a few holiday essentials you know you'll need. If you can get by with just a few pairs of shoes, you'll save space as well as baggage weight.

## Do Your Research

Travellers tend to fall into one of two camps: those who love to plan and map out every moment, and those who prefer to be spontaneous. Even if you are a free spirit who wants to wake up each day and be free to discover whatever comes your way, a little advance research can help you to make the most of your limited vacation time and budget.

Arriving informed means you won't be stuck wondering where all the fun stuff is, and you'll know how much cash you need so you can splurge on something special. A good guidebook or an hour spent surfing the online travel sites before you go can really help you highlight some spectacular places, restaurants, historical sites or current events that you might otherwise miss. It also helps you to narrow down the world of opportunities to those you will enjoy most.

## Like a Good Boy Scout

Being prepared can also help you to avoid nasty surprises, such as unexpected fees and charges. Pack your own bagel to take to the airport waiting lounge so you're not stuck paying $9 for the stale airport variety. Check out the parking situation at your hotel before automatically signing up for a rental car. You might be better off walking and taking the odd taxi to get around.

Hotel review sites such as www.TripAdvisor.com can also prepare you for any unanticipated costs at your hotel or around your destination, as well as alerting you to great inexpensive finds in the area. If you can avoid unexpected expenses, you will have more to spend on fun things . . . such as shopping!

## Father Knows Best

There's a reason Dad liked taking the kids back to Disney World. Sometimes, the best vacation is not being an intrepid traveller: it's about going to a place where you know everyone can relax and have a good time, and you know just what to expect and where to find good value. Comfort and relaxation are worth a lot, especially on a family vacation. Travelling like an old pro gives you a chance to soak up everything your favourite vacation spot has to offer. And isn't that what happy vacations are all about?

# 7

## Buy More Toys

*A great car is important, but what you really want to shoot for is a motorhome pulling a truck, pulling a trailer with two ATVs inside (and possibly a boat, too). Then you'll know you've arrived—and you can arrive on any terrain you want!*

Canadians certainly know how to live the good life. Maybe it's the cold winters that fire up our imagination when it comes to ways to part with our cash, or maybe it's all that cottage time in the summer that gets our spending juices flowing. Either way, we can be a hard-*par-tay-ing* bunch and we're not shy about throwing down our credit cards to prove it.

Surprised? Of course you are. We Canadians prefer to think of ourselves as a modest, mild-mannered group, not prone to conspicuous consumption or keeping up with the Joneses. We're more Clark Kent than Superman, right? We like the simple things in life. We're not like those big-shot Americans.

Ha, we say! Ha! Canadians can spend with the best of 'em, and a global survey by American Express Business Insights[1] has the data to prove it. Following the 2008 financial-market crash, Canadian banks withstood the storm and our economy did not fare as badly as those of the United States or Europe. We lost fewer jobs, relatively speaking. We maintained our access to our big lines of credit. For appearance's sake, we did slightly cut back on splurging—for awhile—and the luxury sector in Canada was down by 9 per cent in 2009, compared to a drop of 14 per cent in the United States and 10 per cent in Europe. The difference is, Canadians got right back up to speed. Our spending on luxuries has increased each year since 2009. Whereas, four years later, people in the States and Europe are still not ready to spend as much on luxuries as they did before the recession.

---

 **IT'S IN THE BAG**

Some products are recession-proof and women's arm candy seems to be one of them. Professors from the University of Southern California Marshall School of Business did a study on how Louis Vuitton and Gucci handbags were marketed and branded before and after the recession.[2] The conventional wisdom at the time was that the age of the conspicuous consumer was dead. Given the way top luxury brands tune their products to suit changing consumer tastes, you

*(continued)*

---

[1] American Express Business Insights, "The Luxe Life," Press Release, Canada News Wire (website), June 19, 2012, http://www.newswire.ca/en/story/995667/the-luxe-life-canada-outpaces-u-s-and-europe-in-luxury-spend-growth.

[2] Ben Steverman, "Conspicuous Consumption Is Back," *Bloomberg BusinessWeek* (website), January 27, 2012, http://www.businessweek.com/investor/content/jan2011/pi20110127_382340.htm.

would expect to see more subtle branding and fewer in-your-face logos, right? So very wrong. Between January 2008 and May 2009, logos on Gucci and Vuitton bags became even bigger and more prominent. Product ads for Burberry were more boldly branded than ever before. The professors concluded that "a good chunk of America loves using products to signal their status." For those who still had the means to shop, they wanted the brand stamps to prove it. Turns out conspicuous consumption never dies, it just gets blingier. (By the way, who knew you could go to university and study handbags? Wow! We really picked the *wrong* major.)

## Honey, Look What We Can Afford

Analysts are saying we are in the midst of a luxury boom. A combination of low interest rates (translated as cheap borrowing costs) and escalating home values over the past decade have made Canadians feel richer. Those fancy things look more affordable today than they ever did before and not because we have more income or cash flow. It would seem that if Canadians have the opportunity to borrow more money, even against their home, they will take it. And usually they will be seen driving around town in it. Between 2001 and 2011, luxury vehicle sales in Canada soared by 67 per cent.[3] In 2012 alone, they jumped 13.2 per cent. Interestingly, www.TransUnion .com reported that car loans in 2012 *also* jumped 13.2 per cent.[4] Coincidence? We think not.

---

[3] Greg Keenan, "Luxury Car Sales Accelerate on Pricing," *The Globe and Mail* (website), May 20, 2012, http://www.theglobeandmail.com/report-on-business/luxury-car-sales-accelerate-on-pricing/article4197765.

[4] Jason Heath, "Who Should Buy a Porsche?" *Financial Post* (website), October 6, 2012, http://business.financialpost.com/2012/10/06/why-you-should-think-twice-about-buying-that-luxury-car.

**LADIES, LET ME HEAR YOU ROAR**

Traditionally, buying flashy new sports cars was a man's game. Not anymore. After many years of accounting for a mere 1 per cent of Ferrari sales in North America, women are now buying 10 per cent of the Ferraris sold here. In China, up to 30 per cent of Ferrari purchases are made by women.[5]

## Diagnosing Affluenza

It sneaks up on you. You are having a perfectly lovely evening, cuddled up with your honey on the sofa watching a movie. You have a glass of your favourite wine and a bowl of hot popcorn. The kids are tucked in their beds. The cat is purring at your feet. All is peaceful on the home front. Yet something in the movie caused a little disturbance in the back of your mind. Maybe it was the house the characters lived in—that clean, cool, ultra-modern dream home with the infinity pool overlooking the valley. Maybe it was the sexy Alfa Romeo in which the suave hero tore around the countryside. Maybe it was the dangle of a diamond earring as the lady love interest strolled down the stairs into the Las Vegas casino.

The gap between what we see on the screen and how we live in reality is a common cause of "affluenza"—that uneasy, envious feeling that we would be happier and more successful if only we had more stuff: a bigger house, a cooler car or fancier clothes.

[5] Courtney Reagan, "Luxury Goods: Men Buying Like Women, Ladies Shopping Like Guys," CNBC (website), March 1, 2012, http://www.cnbc.com/id/46576887/Luxury_Goods_Men_Buying_Like_Women_Ladies_Shopping_Like_Guys.

Wikipedia defines "affluenza" as:

1. A painful, contagious, socially transmitted condition of overload, debt, anxiety and waste resulting from the dogged pursuit of more;

2. The bloated, sluggish and unfulfilled feeling that results from efforts to "keep up with the Joneses."[6]

The desire to grow and achieve more is a natural part of the human condition. As we learn more, work harder and achieve our goals, we aspire not only to *be* more, we also aspire to *have* more. The great irony is that psychologists tell us that the comfortable state of being ultimately yields much greater personal satisfaction than the state of having. The trouble is that we are all consumers and it's this blurring of having and being that leads to the unhealthy condition of affluenza.

## There Is a Cure

The cure for affluenza is to use its power for good. When you find yourself mentally equating having something with being, do a little more thinking about what that new state of being will really look like. Too often, people think themselves into a new acquisition by focusing only on the positive outcomes and brushing off the downsides.

For example, you might think to yourself, if you were to have a boat, you would become the cool guy at the cottage—you know, the guy with the fancy boat. You would become a boat-owner. You equate getting the boat with becoming another kind of cooler, wealthier-looking, fun-loving person.

---

[6] "Affluenza," *Wikipedia* (website), n.d., http://en.wikipedia.org/wiki/Affluenza.

On the positive side, if you make it a goal to save up for a boat, achieve that goal (without sacrificing your other, longer-term financial goals) and pay cash to buy a well-priced, well-maintained, slightly used model, you may very well end up being that happy boat guy. However, what if you can't afford to buy the boat right now? You don't have anything saved for it, you don't even have your emergency fund in place, and you haven't even thought about retirement savings this year. You have a good job and your cash flow is okay—you're able to make all your monthly debt payments—but you don't have a lot left over at the end of the month. Can you still get the boat?

You could. You might look into getting a loan or line of credit to finance the purchase. Your monthly debt payments will increase, adding to your stress each month. And your boat will cost you more than the sticker price, due to the interest you'll have to pay. In short, it will cost you more than planned and it might take you years to pay for it, preventing you from using new money you earn for retirement savings or for investing in new opportunities. On top of that, you will have to come up with more money from your dwindling cash flow for maintenance and repair costs. But hey! You've got a boat and who cares if it seems more like the boat owns you, rather than the other way around? Out there on the water, you will look like a cool, wealthy, fun-loving guy. But like the proverbial duck, you will be paddling like heck underneath the surface to maintain that calm illusion.

In other words, while becoming the boat-owning guy at the cottage, you are also becoming that heavily debt-burdened guy. Heavily debt-burdened guy tends to wake up in the middle of the night sweating over the tsunami of bills he needs to figure out how to pay. Heavily debt-burdened guy snaps at his kids and his family when they ask to go out for burgers because he is stressed about paying for the boat, the cars, the mortgage, the school fees and everything else. Heavily debt-burdened guy is a lot less fun-loving and easygoing than he appears to be.

We're not saying you can't have the boat. If you can save up and buy the boat without impairing your financial goals, then give us a call and we'll be the first ones strapping on our water skis. If, however, your boat-buying aspirations will cause you deep financial stress and sleepless nights, try to make the mental association between new boat and colossal debt burden—and you'll be able to stop affluenza in its tracks.

## Anti-Affluenza Tips

If you find yourself trapped in a state of desperately desiring the latest, greatest thing that your neighbours just bought (or put themselves into debt for), here are a few tips to help you overcome the dreaded affluenza bug.

### Tip #1: The Answer Lies Within (Your Garage)

Take a closer look at all you have already accumulated. Mine your own treasures and breathe new life into your existing possessions. If you're done with them, clear them out to create a cleaner space.

### Tip #2: Be a Late Adopter

Buying the latest gadgets at the top of the market is for suckers. Let other people work out the kinks while you wait for a sale.

### Tip #3: One In, One Out

It's all about balance. If you must buy something new, remove the outdated version and give it a good home with a family that needs and will appreciate it.

### Tip #4: Just Try Saving Instead

For a month, try pocketing the money that otherwise gets spent on your whims. What otherwise goes toward magazines, shoes, movies and dinners out could quickly add up to the price of a Caribbean getaway.

### Tip #5: Let Your Home Evolve

Do you see only what needs to be bought, fixed or replaced rather than what you've already achieved? The beauty of a home is that it reflects your changing style and growing family. Don't be in a rush to perfect your rooms; let them evolve naturally to reflect the layers of your life.

### Tip #6: Healthy Always Looks Good

No anti-aging cosmetics or expensive outfits can cover up a grumpy, tired and stressed disposition. If you want to improve your looks, take your vitamins, go for a run and watch a funny movie with your favourite people.

### Tip #7: Understand Diminishing Utility

The more you consume, the less satisfaction the next bit of consumption will give you. Take a break from accumulating for awhile, so that when you do buy yourself a treat, the enjoyment is richer.

### Tip #8: Enjoy the State of Desire

If you could simply have everything you wanted, you might be surprised at how dull acquiring things would feel. Learn to enjoy and take pleasure in the anticipation of setting goals and achieving them.

## The Monthly Payment Trap

You can just never get ahead. Every time you think you might have a little extra cash on hand, something always comes up and, just like that, it's gone. Sound familiar? You could be stuck in the monthly payment trap. This is a vicious cycle that begins when you start the process of buying things on credit that you should have saved up for and bought outright to begin with. With the interest charges piling up, month after month, you end up paying more for the item than it originally cost and for a much longer time than you anticipated.

---

**⚿ GOLDEN RULE: KNOW YOUR OPPORTUNITY COST**

You can justify your purchases a million ways. But there is always an opportunity cost. Every expenditure that seems so vitally important to your happiness, your success or your personal well-being comes at the price of saving that money for something else longer term. It's the challenge of immediate versus delayed gratification. Before you spend your cash or plunk down that credit card, recognize that you're making an economic choice and think about what future options you may be giving up.

---

All the monthly payments (car loan, student loan, mortgage or rent, condo fees, credit card balances, utility bills, payment plans for phones, gadgets, furniture or other luxuries, memberships, subscriptions and so on) add up to so much that your monthly paycheques get squeezed completely dry. As a result, you have no new cash to apply to lowering your debt and no cash to pay for any new expenditure that comes up. You have barely enough to pay the monthly minimum and keep the whole ship afloat. You become more reliant on debt than ever.

If only you had one monthly payment obligation, perhaps that would be easy enough—which is why debt consolidation is so attractive to people who find themselves drowning in multiple debt payments. And while debt consolidation can help to keep it all organized, it does little if you don't address the root of the problem: how to spend less and save more. (Good thing you're reading this book!)

---

### 🔑 GOLDEN RULE: GET YOUR *FIGHT CLUB* ON

Okay, we're obviously not advocating blowing up the global credit card headquarters as a means of eliminating debt. (C'mon, they've all got backup data systems—you'd still owe the money anyway!) But when you feel a case of affluenza coming on, think of Tyler Durden, as played by Brad Pitt in the film *Fight Club:* "Advertising has us chasing cars and clothes, working jobs we hate so we can buy shit we don't need." We find thinking about Brad Pitt to be helpful in many situations in life, but maybe that's just us.

---

### Defining "Affordable"

The illusion of affordability is like kryptonite to many otherwise fiscally prudent Canadians. It's amazing how retailers, salespeople and even some bankers can tap away at their calculators and computers, and then show you how to make this huge new purchase affordable through low, easy, monthly payments. The lure of the "low, easy, monthly payments" explains why the average Canadian's debt load is now 163 per cent of their disposable income.[7] Just because a bank will give you a loan and you can juggle things around in order to

---

[7] Statistics Canada, "National Balance Sheets Accounts, Second Quarter 2012," *The Daily* (website), October 15, 2012, http://www.statcan.gc.ca/daily-quotidien/121015/dq121015a-eng.htm.

make the payments doesn't mean you can afford to make a particular purchase. Their loan to you might just mean you are building a mountain of debt that at some point—if interest rates rise, or your income slips or some other emergency expenses pop up—could all come crashing down.

So let's look at what you can *truly* afford in order to live a comfortable, happy, not-lying-awake-in-the-middle-of-the-night kind of life. As we explained in Chapter 1, your total debt-to-income ratio (also known as total debt-service-ratio) should never exceed 40 per cent. The ratio is calculated by adding up your monthly debt payments and obligations, and then dividing them by your gross monthly income. Multiply by 100 to get a percentage.

 **HEY, BIG SPENDERS!**

Contrary to conventional wisdom, women are no longer to blame for the family shoe-shopping indiscretions. According to luxury shoe designer Christian Louboutin, the thrill of owning something beautiful knows no gender boundaries. He claims the "demand for men's shoes has been growing incredibly fast."[8] So who are these well-heeled men? We're looking at you, Gen-Xers (those born between 1961 and 1981). In 2011, 60 per cent of all Gen X Canadian luxury shoppers were *men*.[9] We saw those shopping bags hiding in your gym bag. Oh yes, we did!

[8] Courtney Reagan, "Luxury Goods: Men Buying Like Women, Ladies Shopping Like Guys," CNBC (website), March 1, 2012, http://www.cnbc.com/id/46576887/Luxury_Goods_Men_Buying_Like_Women_Ladies_Shopping_Like_Guys.

[9] American Express Business Insights, "The Luxe Life," Press Release, Canada News Wire (website), June 19, 2012, http://www.newswire.ca/en/story/995667/the-luxe-life-canada-outpaces-u-s-and-europe-in-luxury-spend-growth.

## Oh, Those Crazy Kids!

Canadian Gen-Ys (born roughly between 1982 and 2002) have purchasing power and they are not afraid to use it. This group is leading the way when it comes to spending on luxury items. Between 2009 and 2011, in the midst of a global recession, this group increased its spending on luxury fashion by 33 per cent, spent 74 per cent more on travel, and increased its spending on fine dining by 102 per cent (sorry, Mom!). The size of this generation's transactions tends to be smaller than that of its elders (think gadgets, sports gear, clothes and entertainment) but its purchases are plentiful . . . and growing.[10]

So where are these seemingly rich kids getting their cash? It would seem, they're not using cash at all, and when it comes to saving up to buy a luxury item—*fuggedaboudit!* More than half of 18-to-34-year-old Canadian credit card holders are not paying off their balance in full each month, and about 40 per cent are merely making their minimum monthly payment. Furthermore, 23 per cent have been known to miss their monthly payments, 18 per cent are using their credit card to supplement their income and 14 per cent are "routinely maxing out one credit card and needing another as back-up."[11]

Uh-oh. It would seem that we have a generation of young people who have taken online gossip Perez Hilton's aphorism, Fake it 'til you make it, a little too seriously.

 **GADGET CULTURE**

There was a time when conspicuous consumption was expressed through fancy cars, multiple homes, furs and jewellery. And, of course, the big, kick-butt RV. Today, however, we have so many more,

*(continued)*

---

[10] Ibid.

[11] TD Canada Trust, "Play Your Cards Right: Pay It Now or Pay for It Later," TD Canada Trust (website), June 19, 2012, http://www.smrmediaroom.ca/TDCreditCardsAndYou.html.

tiny, complicated, digital forms of luxury. According to advisers at www.MasterCardAdvisors.com,[12] even throughout the recession, people of all income levels somehow managed to keep upgrading their technology and electronics. High-end televisions, mobile phones and iPads keep everyone hungry for constant accumulation.

## In Whose Best Interest?

Our society has become more permissive of debt than ever before. Low interest rates have encouraged Canadians to borrow and spend, rather than save. And boy, are we spending. In Canada, consumer spending accounts for almost 60 per cent of our economy or GDP (gross domestic product).[13]

It is tempting to believe that interest rates will remain low forever. Interest rates were in the double digits throughout the 1980s and into the mid-1990s, when they began dropping down to the levels we see today.

The Gen-Ys will not recall when mortgage rates in Canada hit 20 per cent in 1981.[14] If you had to renew your mortgage at that time, you might have found it costing you double what it cost five years earlier.

Fingers crossed, we will never again have to live with interest rates in the range of 15–20 per cent. However, it is pretty darn

[12] Ben Steverman, "Conspicuous Consumption Is Back," *Bloomberg BusinessWeek* (website), January 27, 2012, http://www.businessweek.com/investor/content/jan2011/pi20110127_382340.htm.

[13] "Household Final Consumption Expenditure, etc. (% of GDP) in Canada," TradingEconomics.com (website), n.d. http://www.tradingeconomics.com/canada/household-final-consumption-expenditure-etc-percent-of-gdp-wb-data.html.

[14] Allan, "History Making Canadian Interest Rates," *RateSuperMarket.ca* (Blog), November 10, 2011, http://www.ratesupermarket.ca/blog/history-making-canadian-interest-rates.

conceivable that over the next few years, interest rates will inch up. It would not be shocking to one day see interest rates of 5–7 per cent. If that doesn't sound so bad to you, keep in mind that it could easily double or triple the cost of your monthly debt payments.

## Charging Those Little Costcentres

Kids often are bigger conspicuous consumers than anyone. They *need* the right brands, they *must have* the right toys. They are hugely influenced by what their friends are wearing and by what products their favourite celebrities and sports stars are flogging. How do you balance treating your little ones to the goodies they crave while getting them to understand the cost of things and the value of money? As they grow up to be teens and young adults, how will they understand that credit cards are not simply a handy extension of their income unless somebody teaches them how interest works? We've got a few ideas to help get you started:

1. **Make 'em pay.** How do you get your kids to stop taking for granted the cost of their incessant-texting lifestyle? Get them to help pay for it, of course. No matter how old they are, they can pay for their apps out of their allowance, or by earning the money through chores. When they are old enough to understand the figures (i.e., old enough to text!), show them the monthly mobile bill and expect them to pay for a portion of their texting charges out of their allowance (or the whole thing if they are old enough to have a part-time jobs). If they can't make the payment, you keep the phone until the bill is paid. It's amazing how much more prudent they will be when it's their own money on the line.

2. **The family that saves together stays together.** When you're planning a big purchase for the family—maybe a new car, a barbecue for the backyard or a family trip—make it a family

effort and reinforce the concept that savings = reward. Create a family savings jar, or get the kids to paint a chart to hang on the kitchen wall depicting the cost of the item, how much money you have saved so far and how much more to go. Get the kids into the spirit of making financial decisions—such as skipping the trip to the new frozen-yogurt shop—so you can put the saved money toward your family goal.

3. **Be a leader.** The best way to teach your kids how to live within their means is to set an example in your own life. If you make them save up to buy their own iPod Touch, the lesson will be lost if you yourself go out and buy an iPad on credit. Show them how you pay off your monthly credit card debt and the importance of getting the balance to zero each month.

---

⚷ GOLDEN RULE: TALK ABOUT REALITY

Your family is prey to the same depictions of typical families and everyday people on television and in movies that you are. Fictional lifestyles that would require millions to achieve in reality set your kids up for feelings of inadequacy. So how do you help your family deal with the symptoms of affluenza? Talk openly about the difference between what they see on the screen and what you deal with every day. Take the time to find out the cost of some of the possessions flaunted by those Kardashians and use it as a chance to teach your kids about income levels and affordability. Be a critical viewer and teach your kids to be the same. It's never too early to learn about living happily within your means!

---

## Are We Spoiling Your Mellow Mood?

Come on, we hear you say, lighten up! The house is worth oodles more than what we paid for it, and as much as we love our folks and want them to grow nice and old, we may just be lucky enough to inherit a nice nest egg on which we can retire. Why worry? Doesn't the government want us to spend and not save in order to keep the economy running? Isn't that why it keeps interest rates so low? Why *not* buy the big Winnebago if the bank is willing to lend us the dough? Why *shouldn't* we all wear beautiful leather shoes hand-stitched by Italian nuns? Why *not* let the kids spend while they are young enough to enjoy it?

By all means, if you have an income sufficient to support your spending habits—then enjoy it! Go crazy. Our goal is to help you understand the difference between sustainable spending that allows you to build wealth and one day be able to stop working and retire gracefully—and spending that will make you go broke.

Those who live large and live on debt end up getting crushed by debt. Just ask the millions of Americans who bought homes they couldn't afford simply because the banks were willing to loan them the funds—and then ended up homeless. Just ask jailed Ponzi-schemers like Bernie Madoff, who created the illusion of billions of dollars of wealth by continually using borrowed money to pay off what was owed to others.

Don't let this be you. Live within your means. Live in the now. Think about Brad Pitt...

# 8

## Pay More When You Can

*Rather than worrying about saving a dollar here and there, just do what is most convenient. Coupons, shopping around and waiting for things to go on sale is such a pain—and why bother for only a few dollars? After all, time is money!*

You've heard their stories. Maybe you've even met them. The guy on your hockey team. The receptionist at your office. The chatty barista at Starbucks where you pick up your morning latte. We're talking about those people who *you know* earn less money than you do, yet they seem to be so much better off than you are—financially speaking, anyway. They own their own homes: maybe a house in the burbs, maybe a condo downtown. They have cars. They have kids they feed, clothe and educate. They take holidays. They look healthy and even happy. If they have your monthly panic attack over paying the bills, it never shows.

How is it that the fellow at your office—the one who earns the same salary as you do—is able to raise five kids on it? His wife manages the brood from home, they live in a charming house and they drive all those kids around in a great big van. Every summer they take a trip out east to visit the grandparents. How is that guy able to make ends meet, with all his obvious financial commitments, and not be stressed about money, while you feel like you can barely get by on the same income?

The answer is that when it comes to salaries, it's not the size that matters, *it's the way you use it.*

## If You Don't Track it, You Can't Manage It

Making a budget is so boring, right? Who wants to live life according to a spreadsheet? Not you, not us. So don't. You heard us: don't. You don't need no stinkin' budget telling you what to do—you already know what you *should* be doing. What you might not be fully clear on at this point is what you *are* doing. Every day.

For one month, keep a tally of everything you spend. We mean everything. Major obvious things, such as mortgage payments; smaller, seemingly inconsequential things, such as a pack of gum or a subway token; and unexpected costs, such as a parking ticket or an impulsive splurge on an online cashmere sale. No two months will be identical, of course, but your habits don't vary too much from month to month. Think that cashmere binge was a rarity? Really? Check last month's credit card bill. Oh, *right.* There was that day you went into HomeSense to pick up some beach towels for the kids to take to camp and you came out with three sets of Egyptian cotton sheets and a new duvet cover. Conveniently forgot about that, didn't you?

Where *is* your money going? Even if you're not prone to accidental shopping sprees, it is very common for people to go through the motions of their daily lives blithely spending money here and there (and well, everywhere) without being conscious of how it's adding up. Parking meters, magazines, yoga classes, coffees and snacks, leaving the lights on, cell phones for everyone in the family, texting and apps for all those phones, cable channels we don't watch and land telephone lines we stopped using five years ago.

If you can spend one month tracking every little expense, we promise you will find some very easy and obvious points where you could have put money into savings instead, as well as areas you could cut in order to liberate more cash flow.

### Where the Heck Does It All Go?

Using Statistics Canada data from 2009, online household budget helper www.Mint.com estimated that "after taxes, pension and insurance payments, gifts and charitable contributions, Canadian households have on average $50,734 dollars annually to spend on everything else in life, from necessities like food and shelter, to the fun stuff like books and booze."[1] Here is a breakdown of where our income goes:

- The roof over your head: 27.8 per cent

- Household operations (including utilities): 6.8 per cent

- Household furnishings and equipment: 3.7 per cent

- Transportation: 19.2 per cent

- Food: 14.3 per cent

- Recreation: 7.6 per cent

- Clothing: 5.6 per cent

- Health care: 4 per cent

- Alcohol and tobacco: 3 per cent

---

[1] Ross Crooks, "Where Are All Those Canadian Dollars Going?" *MintLife* (blog), July 1, 2011, http://www.mint.com/blog/trends/where-are-all-those-canadian-dollars-going.

- Education: 2.4 per cent
- Personal care: 2.4 per cent
- Miscellaneous: 2.3 per cent

*Maclean's* magazine went a little further to see more precisely how some of that household money is spent each year.[2] Keep in mind, the following are averages—and if you find yourself above average, well, let's just hope you have the income to accommodate that!

- Restaurants: $2,066
- Clothes: $1,991
- Alcohol: $905
- Pets: $420
- Fruit and vegetables: $418
- Home technology: $400
- Junk food: $337
- Lottery tickets: $155
- Coffee and tea: $115

## Get an App for That!

Canadians have no problem with spending money online. In fact, more than 80 per cent of all Canadians shop online.[3] We buy our concert tickets online, book our vacations online, order our books online and even, increasingly, our clothing and shoes. (Hey, if we

---

[2] Tamsin McMahon, Nicholas Kohler and Andrew Stobo Sniderman, "How Canadian Are You?" *Maclean's*, June 28, 2012, http://www2.macleans.ca/2012/06/28/how-canadian-are-you.
[3] YStats.com, "2012 North American B2C E-Commerce Report," March 2, 2012, http://ystats.com/en/reports/preview.php?reportId=925.

can avoid the dreaded swimsuit change-room experience, we'll buy our bikinis online too!)

Yes, the interweb is proving to be a mighty convenient tool when it comes to spending our money; often it even saves us a few dollars as we do it. But what about helping us keep more of our money in our wallet—can the interweb help us with that too?

Personal financial management (PFM) websites are geared to do exactly that: they help you track your expenses, calculate and analyze your spending habits and, in some cases, provide real-time transaction reports. You can even set budget limitations and schedule email alerts to notify you when you reach your limit (*beep, beep, beep* . . . Back away from the Apple store!)

A PFM is like a personal bookkeeper that can help you see exactly where and how your money is going. Balancing your chequebook? How passé. Step into the twenty-first century of budgeting with these digital banking tools:

- **Transaction categorization.** Group similar transactions into common categories, such as "travel" or "utilities." By linking to your online banking accounts, your debit and credit card transactions are automatically sorted into these categories, giving you an idea of how you are allocating your cash every month.

- **Budget limits.** You can set maximum spending limits, not only for your spending overall but within different spending categories. For example, you might set a limit of $200 per month on entertainment expenses. An email alert notifies you when you've reached your limit. You may find this much more effective than relying on that little voice inside your head—you know, the one that is way too much of a pushover on many occasions?

- **Manual option.** For those who don't wish to link their bank accounts to an outside website provider, there are manual PFMs that allow you to enter your own data. The PFM then neatly pulls your data together to create spending results analyses.

- **Cash flow management.** Set up parameters for your bank account. When it drops below a certain level—*Alert, alert!* This helps you to avoid that awkward feeling when you look at your account, shriek that you've been a victim of identity theft ("It's in overdraft already?"), but then realize that, no, it was only you.

- **Real-time tracking.** No need to set aside time for the arduous task of going through your monthly expenses. Let your PFM follow you around through your phone and it will keep track of every cent you spend.

- **Bill payment notification.** Set up a notification system to alert you to any recurring payments you need to make. Never miss a bill payment, never have to pay an extra interest fee again!

- **Investments alignment.** Link in your investment accounts and if you have automatic withdrawals coming out of your banking account and going into savings, this will get monitored too. Might as well track the good behaviour while you're tracking the bad, no?

- **Joint expenses.** If you are trying to manage your expenses with a spouse or a roommate, some PFMs will allow you to set up a joint project area where you can keep track of multiple payments and incomes.

- **Savings advice.** Most sites go beyond tracking and give you a customized report identifying areas where you can save more cash or reduce debt more quickly.

- **Tax deductions.** Keep track of tax-deductible expenses and payments simply and easily—no more slogging through messy envelopes of receipts every year.

- **Visual aids.** Some people are just more visual than others. Most PFMs have the ability to translate your data into colourful charts and graphs that can help you to visualize what portion of your money you are spending where.

 **SIX POPULAR PFMS IN CANADA**

There are hundreds of PFMs that Canadians can choose from, and your online bank probably has its own version to boot. Here are a few sample sites that you can check out and look for the features that suit you best. While many of these sites are free, keep in mind that PFMs are like Facebook: if you're not paying a price for a product, then you (and your data) *are* the product.

- RBC (MyFinanceTracker)
- BMO (MoneyLogic)
- www.Mint.com
- www.MoneyTrackin.com
- www.BudgetPulse.com
- www.MoneyStrands.com

## Nutritional Value per Dollar

According to Statistics Canada, the average family household spends between $6,000 and $7,000 on food expenses every year. That's roughly $500 a month. The big question is: What kind of food are you buying? The rising obesity rates indicate that we spend a large proportion of our food budget at restaurants—eating out and on junk food.

Be wary, too, of all those carefully clipped coupons and daily-deal bargains. The discounted items typically are the elaborately packaged processed food from supermarkets and fat-laden goodies from takeout restaurants. When was the last time you saw a coupon for a head of lettuce or a bunch of bananas? Remember: food is your family's fuel. If you feed them healthier, simpler dishes, rather than expensive takeout and processed foods, everyone will function a lot more smoothly and sweetly. Start thinking about how much *nutrition* you're buying with every food dollar.

## Grocery Guru: Three DOs

While you obviously can't cut food out of your monthly budget, there are ways that you can avoid draining your bank account every time you need to grab a carton of milk. Here are our top three suggestions:

### 1. DO Know Your Prices

How many times have you been shocked by the price of toilet paper? It's like the film *Groundhog Day* every time you're in the paper products aisle.

You probably have a core grocery list—the same essential items you buy every time you head out to stock up. You need these items and so you may not look closely at the price: you have to get them, so why bother getting stressed about the price, right? Hands up! What do a dozen eggs cost at your grocery store? A litre of milk? Anyone? *Anyone?*

If you're serious about saving, consider keeping a cheat sheet of prices for the groceries you always buy and those you like to buy when they are on sale. Not only is such a list helpful when you're cruising through the grocery aisles with mind fog, it also helps you to be more aware of whether that free-range chicken is actually a good deal (a cue to stock up now) or merely a promotion for the store (skip it and focus on what you really need).

### 2. DO Shop Around

Comparison shopping is a lot easier when you know what you're paying in the first place (see above). Once you are familiar with the price of your favourite products, you will be amazed at the wide range of prices that different stores will charge for *the same items.* Blindly paying top dollar for a product week after week could end up costing you hundreds of unnecessary dollars. Here's an example: at your neighbourhood grocery store, you may pay $6 for a bottle of dishwashing detergent. Would you still pay $6 if you knew that, just a few blocks away, you could buy the same bottle for $3.99 or even $2 on occasion? Sure, it's just a few bucks, but when you think that a dozen or more items in your cart could each be a few dollars cheaper, suddenly you're talking real money.

Comparing prices between your local pharmacy and a couple of nearby grocery stores is an eye-opening experience. Comparing prices against those in a big box store (like Costco), a bargain retailer (such as Winners or Walmart) or a dollar store (such as Dollarama) is a wallet-opening experience.

### 3. DO Your Own Prep

When you buy items like pre-cut fruit, packaged meals and grated cheese, watch out—you pay a premium. Shelling your own shrimp, washing your own lettuce and grating your own cheese save you a ton on your weekly grocery bill (not to mention a load of additives and preservatives). Whole, unprocessed food is much less expensive than packaged and prepared foods.

A head of lettuce is a fraction of the cost of the bagged, pre-washed variety and takes seconds to rinse and tear into a salad. An inexpensive cut of meat, roasted whole, can provide a week of healthier, cheaper and tastier sandwich fixings than packages of processed deli meats.

Takeout often ends up costing as much as going to a restaurant. If you have a busy week ahead and know you won't have time to cook—stock up on staples that are quick to fix (think couscous, pasta, wraps, eggs and soup) and healthy snacks such as granola, yogurt, nuts, cheese and fruit. Skip the high-sodium, high-cost and ultimately unfulfilling frozen dinners. When you have more time, stock the freezer with some of your favourites: homemade waffles for popping in the toaster on weekday mornings; lasagne, casseroles and stews for nights when everyone gets home late and *hungry*.

If you just can't spare the time for the extra prep work to grate your own cheese, then it's time to start putting your partner and kids to work. Meal preparation is prime family bonding time!

 **THE SCENT OF A DINNER**

Even before you walk through the sliding glass door, you can smell it: the wafting aroma of freshly baked bread. Your resolve to lower your carbohydrate intake begins to weaken. Once you enter the store, the juicy sweet smell of roast chicken and barbecue ribs takes over, making your stomach growl and your grocery list go out the window. Grocery store chains spend a lot of money on analysts and behavioural psychologists who design their stores strategically to make the maximum profit off your impulsive reactions. Once you see through the smoke and mirrors (or bread and barbecue), it's easier to avoid these sneaky sales tactics.

## Grocery Guru: Three DON'Ts

Still having trouble keeping your food costs down? Avoid these common supermarket traps:

### 1. DON'T Choose Items from the Middle Kingdom

Items placed at eye level catch your attention first. Retailers are wise to this and typically place the most expensive items front and centre on the middle shelves. For better prices, shift your focus: check out the top and bottom shelves. Similarly, the middle aisles are usually the ones filled with convenience foods and packaged goods. Stick to the perimeter of the store for your fruits, vegetables, meat, fish and fresh bread. Venture into specific middle aisles only on an as-needed basis. The common tactic of strolling up and down every aisle just to see if there's anything you need is a recipe for overspending.

### 2. DON'T Give In to the Kid Factor

When confronted with a toddler meltdown, you might be willing to buy anything just to stop the madness. Kids of all ages (spouses, too, occasionally) can be a challenge in grocery stores. They distract you from your list and the prices of the items you are choosing. They get impatient, leading you to start throwing items in your cart just to get the job done. And sometimes they throw their own highly processed, over-priced favourites into the cart as well. If you can, try to shop without the kids until they are at an age at which you can make the trip an educational and interactive experience, teaching them about food choices and price comparisons.

### 3. DON'T Shop When You're Hungry

It's incredible how a craving for Doritos can sneak up on you. You leave the office or finish up at the gym and you stop at the supermarket to look for ideas for dinner. By the time you get to the checkout, you've got all the ingredients to make a heap of baked nachos, a frozen pizza *and* duck *à l'orange* with crème brûlée for dessert. Plus two new kinds of breakfast cereal and a box of fat-free chocolate coconut bars. Hungry much? When you're starving, *everything* looks good and just the suggestion of a certain dish can stimulate an instant craving. If you find yourself stuck having to go to the supermarket on an empty stomach, grab a (lower-priced) energy bar to munch on while you shop—you can pay for it with your other groceries.

 **THE BIG REVEAL—WHAT'S IN YOUR FREEZER?**

The proof of any great grocery bargain-hunter is a well-stocked freezer. If the food is forgotten, however, those savings are lost. Throwing out freezer-burnt food is throwing out money, pure and simple. Dedicate one day a week as eat-out-of-the-freezer night. Make a concerted family effort to use up what you've got rather than piling new items on top of old. Date and label everything that goes in to avoid those mystery blocks of meat. Most importantly, keep a balance of homemade, quick-fix favourites alongside supplies for those occasions when you have time to really cook.

## Kibble Costs

And you thought feeding yourself was getting expensive. In Canada, the cost of pet care is on the rise. According to the Pet Industry Joint Advisory Council of Canada (PIJAC), the pet industry is worth $8.9 billion and spending on pets is rising by 4.5 per cent each year.[4] The reason, it seems, is that we no longer treat our pets as animals but rather as full-fledged family members.

---

[4] "Cost of Pet Ownership on the Rise," *Toronto Sun*, July 18, 2011, http://www.torontosun .com/2011/07/18/cost-of-pet-ownership-on-the-rise.

According to Statistics Canada, in 2009 the average family spent $870 a year on their pets. Yet the Ontario Veterinary Medical Association advises pet owners that the annual costs are typically much higher. According to their data, caring for a cat can cost you roughly $1,400 per year, and for a dog it's around $1,800 per year. This includes food, insurance, litter and vaccines. (Organic, free-range ground chicken livers and Jimmy Chew dog toys extra.)

## Boozin' on a Budget

If you look a little closer at the stats cited by *Maclean's* magazine earlier in this chapter, the average Canadian spends more on booze than on fresh veggies.[5] Blame our provincial government–controlled liquor stores if you wish, but there are still a few ways you can enjoy a tipple now and then without toppling your monthly finances. Here are five of our favourites:

- **Seasonal sales.** While they may monopolize the market, the liquor stores do try to be kind to your wallet now and then with seasonal sales and promotions on wines or featured products. Pay attention to these markdowns. Often you can pick up a great wine for a few dollars less than usual.

- **BYOB.** Do your research before you book a table at that hot new restaurant. If you call ahead, many restaurants will allow you to bring in your own bottle of wine for the night, charging you a small corkage fee for the privilege. Other restaurants offer special half-price wine nights to encourage weeknight crowds, so be a hipster and get to know your local scene.

---

[5] Tamsin McMahon, Nicholas Kohler and Andrew Stobo Sniderman, "How Canadian Are You?" *Maclean's*, June 28, 2012, http://www2.macleans.ca/2012/06/28/how-canadian-are-you.

- **Think like a student.** Invite everyone over for cocktails *before* heading out for dinner or a show. This is fondly known among college kids as the "pre-game warm-up." There are some traditions we never grow out of, thankfully. When seemingly mature adults drink at home before going out, they class it up with a few oven-baked canapés and call it a *"cinq à sept."*

- **Home brew.** An off-brand bottle of vodka becomes something special when you've infused it with lavender from your garden. Invigorate cheap bourbon with citrus slices and vanilla bean. Make your own version of popular liqueurs such as Baileys Irish Cream and Kahlúa and store them in pretty glass bottles. Not only will they cost you a fraction of the store-bought price, but you will gain serious street cred among your foodie and mixologist friends.

- **Duty-free.** It's well worth stocking up on a few bar basics at the duty-free boutique next time you cross the border. While there are limits on the quantity of alcohol you can cart back to Canada before being taxed, many bottles of premium liquor can be picked up for half the domestic price.

---

**⚷— GOLDEN RULE: DON'T BE FOOLED**

Do not be fooled into spending more on so-called value promotions (e.g., buy-three-for-$6 deals). Do the math on the price-per-item first. If stocking up makes sense, then go for it. However, if you really need only one item at $2 instead of five for $10, don't get lured into buying the bulk quantity. At many stores, the sale price applies even to one item (though the advertising promotes the multi-buy). Even if the reduced price doesn't count on a single item, does saving 20 cents on a bag of marshmallows really justify buying five bags? You'll be into s'mores for months . . .

## Bulk It Up

We admit it, we like big carts and we cannot lie . . . Maybe it's our Canadian long-winter mentality, but the notion of stocking our pantries and cold storage rooms with enough supplies to keep our families nourished in the event of a year-long power outage is strangely compelling. In addition to being prepared for freak natural disasters, buying in bulk can save you hundreds, if not thousands of dollars a year on grocery staples such as rice, spices, flour, sugar, nuts, condiments and pasta.

However, much as we love 'em, bulk stores such as Costco, Wholesale Club and even Walmart can become addictive and problematic to your budget in their own unique way. So here are a few of the bulk-buying traps to watch out for.

### More Isn't Always Cheaper

There is a strange phenomenon that often afflicts shoppers when they walk into a bulk store. Perfectly reasonable people are seized by bargain frenzy and find themselves buying 50,000 Q-tips and 10-kilogram tubs of guacamole. The trouble is it can be hard to calculate the price per unit on supersized packages, which means you'll never know whether hauling home a year's worth of toilet paper is actually a cost-saving exercise, or if you'd be better off settling for the understated eight-pack at your corner drugstore. Because many bulk stores buy merchandise directly from suppliers and keep their overhead costs low, they *can* offer lower prices, but that doesn't mean they always do. Get to know your prices and how much you usually spend on these items. When you spot a bulk deal with a lower price per unit, grab it!

### Warning: This Could Affect Your Waistline

Buying the extra-large bag of M&M's might be a bargain—unless, of course, it also leads you to require an upgrade to extra-large pants.

(And no, it probably isn't a coincidence that they have a lot of those for sale, too.) That may sound harsh, but it's true. A research paper published by the University of North Carolina at Greensboro in 2010 found that every time a new Walmart Supercenter was added to a community of 100,000 people, the obesity rate rose by 2.3 per cent. The authors concluded that the proliferation of Walmarts could be a contributing factor in the 10.5 per cent increase in obesity in the U.S. since the 1980s. The big-bottom line is that having larger quantities of food and treats around the house tempts people to *consume* more than they otherwise would. If portion control is an issue for you, tread carefully into the big box store.

### Too Much of a Good Thing

You just bought a 5-kilogram bag of the kids' favourite breakfast cereal, and one and a half kilos in, they decide they no longer like it. In fact, they *hate it* now. It happens. Or maybe you'll get tired of heaving that huge, discount bottle of fabric softener every time you do a load of laundry. Which leads us to another problem with buying things in large quantities: waste. Canadians waste about 183 kilograms of food per person each year, according to the George Morris Centre's 2010 study "Food Waste in Canada." When you buy in bulk, make sure it's something you use a lot and often. If the biggie-size packaging annoys you once you get it home, divvy it up into smaller, normal-size containers to use every day. As for perishable items like meat or yogurt, make sure to use them up before they go bad ("Yogurt meat salad, again? Aw, Mom!").

### Loonie for Dollar Stores

How do they do it? How is it that dollar stores can sell exactly the same name-brand products that you find at Walmart, Costco or

Shoppers Drug Mart, for prices that are on average about 40 per cent cheaper?

Typically, variety stores rely on wholesalers to supply their products, paying the middleman a fee that cuts into their profit margin. The biggest dollar store in Canada, Dollarama, skips this step and sources its products in Asia. This helps them maintain a solid business margin even when they're selling items at ridiculously low prices. For products they sell for $1 each, Dollarama spends between 28 and 30 cents. For premium items selling for $1.50, $2 or $3, Dollarama sources products at a cost of up to 40 cents each.

Across Canada, we have six main dollar-store chains as well as local independent shops and franchisees, totalling about 1,200 dollar stores in all. In addition to Dollarama, we have Everything for a Dollar, Buck or Two Plus!, Your Dollar Store with More and Great Canadian Dollar Store. Each dollar store location in the top six chains serves about 30,000 customers per year. Compare this to the United States, where the top five dollar stores serve only about 14,000 customers per store each year. Clearly, Canadians are loonie for 'em.

## Crazy for Coupons

A lot has changed in the world of couponing. Remember your grandmother sitting down at the kitchen table and casually clipping offers from the local weekly paper? Over time, coupons started showing up on the back of store receipts and inside cereal boxes. Today, there are entire websites and mailing lists dedicated to the sport of coupon collection. If you are keen to get more out of the coupon craze, here are a few tricks of the trade you should know:

- **Coupon-collecting.** Numerous blogs and websites track coupons, freebies and special offers. Depending on how coupon-committed you are, some of them even have forums where you can collaborate, swap and trade tips with other coupon-lovers.

Furthermore, many have email alerts so you don't actually have to check the website daily. Some favourite Canadian deal websites: www.BargainMoose.ca, www.SimplyFrugal.ca and www.SmartCanucks.ca.

- **Coupon-stacking.** This is the practice of using more than one coupon for a single product. It is popular among coupon extremists in the United States, but in Canada the only store that *officially* allows coupon stacking is London Drugs and they have specific guidelines that you can find on their website. Some other stores do allow coupon stacking, they just don't advertise it.

- **Flyer-tracking.** By tracking grocery flyers, you can wait until a product goes on sale before using your coupon—giving you a discount on a discount. How on earth do you keep track of all the grocery store flyers? Online, of course. For example, www.Flyerland.ca offers access to numerous store coupons, flyers and catalogues, and even offers a product search tool.

## What Is Your Coupon Personality?

"Know thyself" is inscribed on the Temple of Apollo at Delphi. But you don't need to trek to Greece to know what kind of coupon style you have. Just for fun, see if you can recognize your attitude when it comes to bagging bargains . . .

✓ **The casual couponer.** Taking a traditional approach, you don't go out of your way to hunt down a discount. If you happen to come across a coupon for items you use often, you grab it. If you know you will be buying a certain item in the near future, you might keep an eye out for sales or coupons, but if you can't find any, it won't stop you from buying what you need.

✓ **The bargain hunter.** You take couponing far more seriously, buying multiple copies of the newspaper if it looks like a good coupon week. You frequently check printable coupon websites and deal aggregators. You usually make your shopping list based on what coupons you have to use up, and you love using a coupon on a sale item for that extra bit of savings.

✓ **The extreme couponer.** You are not only familiar with coupon-stacking and flyer-tracking, they are a part of your daily life. Your pantry or basement may contain 15 boxes of the same cereal, 20 bottles of shampoo and 10 containers of mustard. Family members have suggested that your hobby is bordering on obsessive behaviour. You keep a coupon filing system and may even secretly keep a few receipts as fond keepsakes of particularly successful bargain scores.

## Groupie Love

Group-buying sites, also known as daily deal sites, are a genius invention that brings together the power of social networking, group dynamics and bargain hunting. At last count, there were 1,791 group-buying websites in North America and a total of 9,575 similar sites around the world.[6]

The rationale is simple: if you could spend 50 per cent, 70 per cent or even 90 per cent less on something you would buy anyway, such as a meal at a restaurant or a gym membership, why wouldn't you go for the deal and avoid paying full price? Here are a few examples of group-buying websites that are worth checking out:

- www.SmartBetty.com. Now, this is virtuous spending. Every time you purchase one of Smart Betty's money-saving deals,

---

[6] DailyDealMedia.com.

the company gives 10 per cent of their revenue back to a local charity that you get to choose.

- www.WagJag.com. With myriad shopping categories, WagJag includes a section dedicated to grocery deals. The site is also linked to their partner company, www.Jaunt.ca, which offers great daily deals on travel.

- www.RDeals.ca. This daily deal site is powered by Rogers and is getting bigger every day. Popular deals have included half-off lower bowl seats to the Toronto Raptors and 65 per cent off Android tablets.

- www.Groupon.com. The king of group-buying sites, Groupon is a publicly traded company that was the first to really get the group-buying ball rolling. As a result, its roots run deep in almost every city, where you can find deals when travelling or as gifts for faraway loved ones.

- www.LivingSocial.com. Phat Buddha tattoos? Dance classes? Wine tours? While the site offers all kinds of deals, it really shines when it comes to offering unique services and, well, as the name implies, social experiences.

---

 **SEE YA LATER, AGGREGATOR**

Group-buying pros know that if you don't want to wake up every morning to a crowded email inbox, a daily deal aggregator will collect all the deals available that day and deliver them to you in one efficient email. For example, www.DeliverTheDeals.com provides offers from Groupon, LivingSocial, MadDeal, WagJag and a handful of other great Canadian collective buying websites.

## Paying Less Feels Great

No matter how much you've got in the bank, getting a good deal or a discount always feels great. Scoring a lower price on the essentials you need to buy anyway increases your cash flow mojo and gives you greater spending power. As we said at the beginning of the chapter, it's not how much you earn, it's how you use your limited income—how you stretch it, how you track it and how you get more from it every day.

# 9

## Shop Every Day

*Treat yourself whenever you get the chance. After all, nothing feels better than coming home with something new at the end of a hard day. If you can't find a use for what you've bought, you can always add it to your gift closet. You do have a gift closet, right?*

Shopping has come a long way, baby. You are probably too young to remember, but back in the olden days, when your toaster called it quits, you either had to try to fix it (forget about finding a toaster repairman—that was in the olden *olden* days) or get in your car and drive 20 minutes to the mall, pay for parking, weave your way through crowds of shoppers, stalk back and forth through the housewares department for half an hour trying to find a customer service person to help you, only to eventually learn the toaster you selected from the display shelf is out of stock. The only other toaster that would appeal to you costs $20 more, but at this point you would be so frustrated that you'd pay anything to get this toaster-seeking mission over with so you could get on with your life!

Nowadays, when your toaster dies, you simply crack open a cold one, head over to the computer, log on to Amazon and a few keystrokes later, the exact toaster you want is en route to your house (at a price 30 per cent cheaper than the price offered by your local department store). In less than half an hour you could be done and onto surfing Netflix for a movie to watch.

Online shopping has made the process of buying things so convenient that it is tougher than ever to avoid shopping. You spend hours "researching" items you might want and are more likely to buy them than if you had to physically go to the store and hunt them down. Meanwhile, retailers that occupy stores in the real world have become a lot more sophisticated as well. Market analysts dissect customer data and buying behaviour, while mapping out aisles and shelving displays for maximum subliminal impact.

In this chapter, we're going to look at some of the ways retailers push your buttons so you can be better prepared to push back in a world that seems hell-bent on getting you to part with your hard-earned cash.

---

 **ARE YOU YOUR OWN FINANCIAL CRISIS?**

The global financial crisis stems not only from government over-spending and corporate greed, but also over-leveraged individuals who expected the glory days of low interest rates and unlimited access to credit to continue forever.

Ultimately, your own personal financial stability comes down to you and your propensity to spend. Your credit card does not offer itself up to the cashier, nor does it type its own numbers onto the online checkout. Banks may offer, but they certainly don't force you to take on, a too-big mortgage. If you really want to stabilize your personal

*(continued)*

---

finances, you have the power and the authority to make it happen. Start by enacting a moratorium on overspending and begin bailing yourself out of any debt that you've accumulated. Like, now . . . before the protestors start camping on your front lawn.

## Games Retailers Play

When you enter a store, you are usually so caught up in trying to remember what you came there for (and trying not to get distracted by all the shiny, sparkly things) that you usually fall right into the traps that sneaky retailers love to set for you. Oh, don't feel bad! It would require a degree in behavioural psychology with a minor in marketing data analysis to spot some of these tricks. Let's consider a few:

- **Pricing ploys.** The flyers stuffed in your mailbox are not really designed to advertise cheap goods—they're meant to get you into the store. The store flaunts a "loss leader" (an underpriced item) to entice you to come check it out. Once you are in the store and discover that the $100 surround-sound audio system sounds pretty crappy, you are more likely to look around and find a more expensive sound system you love. Since you went to the store with a mission to buy, you're predisposed to buying the expensive item just to make your shopping trip worthwhile.

- **Rebate runarounds.** Retailers love to offer rebates rather than sale prices. While the promise of a rebate may be enough to convince you to buy an expensive item, there is an excellent chance you won't get around to redeeming it. Often rebates are relatively small and notoriously (and deliberately) difficult to cash in. If it's only $25 (on $500!), you're likely to forget about it or give up at the first hassle you encounter.

- **Two-sided stores.** Stores nearly always position their more expensive, newer items in beautiful displays at the front of the store, with sale items arranged carelessly at the back. This subtly affects your perception of the quality and style of the items you are looking at. Even when you know the store has simply moved the merchandise to make room for the new season's stock, on some level there is a perception that last season's sweater is worth less simply because it is being treated negligently. The higher-priced items at the front *feel* more valuable and their higher cost seems justified because they are displayed with such great care.

- **Impulse grabs.** You're standing in line. You're bored. Thankfully, the retailer has strategically positioned plenty of goodies to keep you interested. You may already have a full cart, but now you are a captive of the queue and have plenty of time to admire the candy, treats, magazines and all kinds of last-chance items to increase the total amount of your shopping bill.

- **Just try it on.** Don't even kid yourself. In 2009, the *Journal of Consumer Research* found that consumers were willing to pay more for items they touched than those they couldn't touch.[1] If you try it on, you are halfway to buying it. If it fits, it's sold. Therefore, if you don't have the cash to buy it, keep your hands to yourself!

- **Not too hot, not too cold.** You prefer the one in the middle, the one that's just right, *right?* Consumers generally act like Goldilocks and nowhere is this more apparent than in the retail sector. If you go to the store to pick up garbage bags, you will see the most expensive brand and think, "That's

---

[1]Sean Gregory, "Want to Save Some Money? Shop Without Touching," *Time,* April 3, 2009, http://www.time.com/time/business/article/0,8599,1889081,00.html.

too expensive. I'm not paying that much for something going in the trash bin." Then you look at the cheapest brand and because it's so cheap, you are skeptical about its quality. You feel safer choosing a brand priced somewhere in the middle. As a result, most retailers will purposely choose similar items at a range of price points to guide you into paying a little more.

- **The illusion of a deal.** Similarly, when retailers want to sell more of a certain product, rather than putting it on sale, they will put a similar, more expensive item next to it. You look at the two toasters, side by side, and you think, wow, this one is half the price of that one! You assume the lower-priced version is a better value simply because it's positioned next to a more expensive version.

- **The power of nine.** You already know that most prices end in a nine, right? You also don't really care about the difference between spending $10 and $9.99. And yet the nines persist because they work—they make you *feel* that the retailer is trying to keep prices as low as possible even when you *know* this isn't the case. Even house prices are listed just under psychological thresholds, with prices such as $498,000 rather than $500,000.

## Cookies: Not as Sweet as They Sound

More than 80 per cent of Canadians shop online[2] and why wouldn't they? Shopping online is super-convenient, you don't get distracted by attempted upsells and you can scour the world for the best price on the item you want. In short, you feel like you have more control. But do you really? How do you know if you are getting the best price?

---

[2] YStats.com, "2012 North American B2C E-Commerce Report," March 2, 2012, http://ystats.com/en/reports/preview.php?reportId=925.

More and more online retailers are using specialized software to help them profile you as you shop. They can figure out whether you are likely to pay more or less. And whether you are in a hurry and just want the quickest, priciest item, or whether you are looking around, deliberating over prices and may be encouraged to buy more if you're offered a discount.

Many websites use cookies embedded in your web browser to track your browsing on the Internet. These websites can use this information to surmise things about you: your age, your income level, your demographic identity. When you browse an online retailer's website, the retailer may be able to see where else you have been shopping and what kind of items you looked at. Your Internet address also gives away your geographical location. All of this information can then be used to customize a price, just for you, based on what the retailer thinks you are likely to spend.

A travel-planning website, www.Orbitz.com, admits to customizing prices this way. It starts by using software to detect if the user is on a Mac or a Windows PC. According to Forrester Research, in the United States, the average household income for adult owners of a PC is $74,452, while a Mac user's is $98.560.[3] Orbitz finds that Mac users are 40 per cent more likely to book a four- or five-star hotel than PC users. Consequently, if you sign onto Orbitz using a Mac, you will see a selection of pricier hotels than you would see on a PC. The company stresses that it does not offer different rates for the same rooms.

However, charging different prices for the same items depending on who you are, where you are from and how much money and time you spend online is a very real outcome that many online

---

[3] Dana Mattioli, "On Orbitz, Mac Users Steered to Pricier Hotels," *Wall Street Journal*, August 23, 2012, http://online.wsj.com/article/SB10001424052702304458604577488822667325882.html.

retailers are tinkering with. According to one industry expert, at least six of the biggest online retailers based in the United States are customizing prices.[4]

## How Do They Know So Much?

Retailers acquire the ability to customize prices by collecting, buying and analyzing an incredible amount of customer data. Every time you swipe your credit card, fill out an online survey, call a customer help line, sign up for a website or return an item, your data is being tracked. Just by knowing your postal code, companies can figure out demographic details, such as the size of your family and the age of its members, your household income, your ethnicity, the kind of pets you own and your proximity to certain shops and services.

Beyond that, things can get pretty personal. Marketing companies that specialize in data collection can figure out specifics such as what credit cards you carry; where you went to school; what jobs you've had; where you've lived; whether you've ever been divorced, declared bankruptcy or had kids; your political interests; how many cars you have; where you donate your money and what kind of topics you search when you're online. (So much for the privacy of your own home!)

The stuff you buy, online or in person, is also tracked, of course. When this data gets aggregated from all the places you shop, a lot can be inferred about you. A company with this information can see that you buy Cheerios in bulk, that you've switched to LED lights and that you prefer Starbucks to Tim Hortons. All this information is then used to entice you to buy those products *at their stores* as well as to predict what other products they might be able to interest you in while you shop with them.

---

[4] "How Deep Are Your Pockets?" *The Economist*, June 30, 2012, http://www.economist.com/node/21557798.

**TARGETED BY TARGET**

A few years ago, a Minneapolis father was going through his mail and was shocked to find coupons from Target addressed to his teenage daughter. The coupons offered discounts on baby clothes and cribs. He angrily accused the store of encouraging a high school student to become pregnant. A few weeks later, he found out that his daughter was, in fact, already pregnant. Who knew that Target would be the first to know?[5]

## First-Time Parents: The Holy Grail

According to retail experts, consumers get very stuck in their shopping ways. Maybe you've always bought your cleaning supplies at Canadian Tire and your toilet paper at Shoppers Drug Mart. You would never buy these items at Loblaws because that is where you get your food. Perhaps you've bought Skippy peanut butter for your whole life and have never considered switching to a different brand. These are hard habits for retailers to break.

However, analysts have found that major life changes disrupt these patterns. Heading to college, getting married, getting divorced, moving homes, changing jobs and, of course, having a child, all shift something in our psyche that makes us open to changing what we consume and how we buy. For retailers, these life-changing moments are huge opportunities to win more of your wallet. Shell-shocked, time-pressed, sleep-deprived first-time parents are the biggest opportunity of all, and big retailers are increasingly aggressive about anticipating their needs and getting them while their brand loyalty may be up for grabs.

[5] Charles Duhigg, "How Companies Learn Your Secrets," *New York Times*, February 16, 2012, http://www.nytimes.com/2012/02/19/magazine/shopping-habits.html?pagewanted=all&_r=0.

## Creepy or Convenient?

You give up privacy for the sake of convenience constantly these days. Facebook might be able to recognize your face (which feels creepy), but you still post pictures of your summer vacation and the kids' costumes at Halloween (convenient). So it might seem creepy that while you're on Facebook an ad pops up promoting a juicer . . . the very same juicer you looked at a few days ago on a different website. However, that juicer is now being offered to you at a 15 per cent discount—well now, that is darned convenient, isn't it?

## The Cashless Society

Just when you thought you couldn't be more in love with your iPhone or BlackBerry, it is poised to become your new digital sugar daddy (or sugar mama, depending on your preference, of course!). We are talking about the virtual wallet, which, of course, contains virtual money. Rather than keeping cash and cards in a physical wallet, all of your payment information will be consolidated electronically and accessed through your smartphone. This means you can take your loot to the counter, tap your phone on a reader, enter a password and you're on your way. Eventually, digital wallets may also hold data such as your driver's licence, health card and library card.

Eek, you say? Worried about all that information gathered in one easy-to-steal place? Not to worry, say the providers of the technology. A wallet can be stolen by any old hack, while stealing the payment information on a smartphone requires serious hacking skills.

## A Personal Reboot

While you mull over the creepy-versus-convenient paradox, there is also the question of how to keep a hold on that cash—whether it's virtual or physical—when there are so many convenient means of being parted from it. Rather than allowing technology to put distance between you and your cash, use that technology to monitor and track your spending, count your savings—and safely stash your money for later.

If you're having a hard time staying on budget and staying out of debt, maybe it's time for a personal finance reboot. Think of it as the equivalent of unplugging your computer and logging on again:

- Check your bank balance and credit card balance online every day to gain awareness of your cash flow levels at all times.

- Download personal financial software or an app to help you track where your money is going each month.

- Give the plastic a rest and use only cold hard cash for awhile. You will have more time to think about what you're buying and actually see the cash you are giving up.

These three steps may seem ridiculously simple, but sometimes going back to basics is the only way to shift us from a bad pattern into a better one. After all, when we talk ourselves into overspending with money we don't actually have, it isn't because we've lost the ability to do simple math. We've just chosen to avoid facing up to our indulgent retail habits.

## Swiping into Submission

Money used to be a tangible asset, one that people counted, carried in their pockets and hid under their mattress. But thanks to credit cards—and, now, electronic payment systems—cash is a rarity. Rather than holding it in our hands and passing it among one another, we exchange it electronically. While this is certainly convenient, it's not such a good thing when it comes to those prone to denying how much they spend.

Studies suggest that using a credit card drastically affects our spending behaviour. Debit cards have a similar—although less powerful—effect. Soon, we will be able to merely wave our iPhone or BlackBerry in the direction of the cash register and out we go. It's just that easy—which, of course, is the problem.

When we go to the bank, withdraw money, see our balance and hold that cash in our hands, it seems real. You can feel, see and smell the money you are giving up in order to gain that item you want to purchase. On the other hand, when you hand over a plastic card which you then return to your wallet, wholly intact, the money you are exchanging doesn't seem real: it's just a number in a computer somewhere. This is why it is so easy to overspend when you don't use cash. You can spend while choosing to remain oblivious to the amounts being siphoned out of your accounts. If one card stops working, you simply switch to another.

 **NO PAIN, NO PURCHASE**

A study published in the journal *Social Psychological and Personality Science* in September 2010 found that luxury purchases, such as designer clothes, watches and nice cars, are more likely to be made with credit cards than cash, especially if they fall into the category of status consumption. In other words, if you buy something you don't need and can't afford, you are more likely to reach for your credit card. If you buy a pair of $60 jeans at the Gap, you might pay cash. If you splurge on a pair of $260 J Brand jeans, you'll probably use your credit card.

## The Joy and Pain of Plastic

You are holding the cashmere sweater—it's so very soft!—and you are seriously considering whether or not to buy it. Psychologically, you are weighing the pleasure of acquiring the item and owning it (how casually sexy you will look while also staying warm!) versus the pain of paying for it (that is $350 you won't be spending on a flight to a ski hill this winter).

The easier the transaction is—a few keystrokes, the swipe of a card, the wave of a smartphone—the less tangible the cost becomes. The money you are spending does not seem real and the painful part of the equation you weighed in your head is over in a few seconds. Transaction approved. Done.

The more swift and impersonal paying for something becomes, the more likely you are to rush out of the store with bags of beautiful things you can't afford—or find yourself inundated by packages containing your online purchases delivered by postal workers and couriers.

---

🔑 **GOLDEN RULE: THE FAMILY GIFT BUDGET**

Hold a family meeting to discuss a family gift budget. Engage everyone in the process so they feel equally committed to the new plan. Mark all family birthdays and gift-giving anniversaries on a calendar that is kept in a central place where everyone can access it. Determine an annual gift budget and assign spending limits to each gift-giving event in order to stay within budget. If you buy gifts ahead of time, make sure you reconcile the budget with what you've spent. Encourage all family members to stay on track with the gift budget throughout the year.

---

## Oops, I Slipped and Dropped My Credit Card…

If you thought retail therapy was your own private guilty pleasure, shove over, because you are certainly not alone. According to the

BMO "Psychology of Spending Report,"[6] 59 per cent of Canadians shop impulsively, spending an average of $3,720 on unplanned purchases each year.

What is it that tempts us? The most common impulse purchases are clothing, dining out, shoes, books and magazines, music, movies and technology gadgets. The majority of people—52 per cent—regret those purchases after the fact. An alarming 42 per cent of Canadians buy items they never even use.

## Mars and Venus Go Shopping

Quick—what comes to mind when you think of impulse shopping? Women buying shoes, right? Sigh. Carrie Bradshaw of "Sex and the City" and her Louboutins set that cliché in stone! However, it turns out that Canadian guys are not immune to the charms of a good shoe either. In fact, men spend *twice* as much on impulse buys as women do. On average, men spend $414 per month, while women spend an average of $207 on unplanned splurges.[7] The top five impulse purchases for men are as follows:

- Dining out
- Clothing
- Books and magazines
- Shoes
- Software and apps

[6] BMO Financial Group, "BMO Psychology of Spending Report," Press Release, September 25, 2012, http://newsroom.bmo.com/press-releases/bmo-psychology-of-spending-report-impulse-shoppin-tsx-bmo-201209250821167001.
[7] Ibid.

The top five impulse purchases for women are:

- Clothing

- Dining out

- Shoes

- Books and magazines

- Cosmetics

 **CREDIT CARDS AND CANDY**

Credit cards and impulsive behaviour are not relegated to the clothing and technology aisles. A study conducted by Cornell University and published in the *Journal of Consumer Research* in June 2011 looked specifically at grocery store purchases. They found that paying with a credit card significantly affected the amount people spent on unhealthy snack-food items. However, the method of payment had virtually no effect on how much people spent on the healthy foods they usually purchased. The researchers concluded that credit cards don't necessarily make you spend more on necessary and planned purchases, but they do make you more likely to grab things you don't need—and spend about 20 per cent more than you would if you paid in cash.

## Are You a Willing Target?

Okay, we hear you saying, but retailers use the same tricks on everyone. Why is it that some people are able to cruise right on by such traps without spending a dime more than what they planned, while other people end up blowing the equivalent of a month's rent on a completely impulsive purchase?

Here's a hint: they don't call it "retail therapy" for nothing. If you find yourself feeling bored, lonely or stressed—maybe you feel that you have no control or authority in some important area of your life—you head out for a walk to innocently pick up some yogurt and what happens? You limp home under the weight of shopping bags, not just yogurt, but also lamb; fresh mint; a Moroccan cookbook; an enamelled, cast-iron tagine pot; a set of linen napkins and a pair of sunglasses—which you totally need because your old ones are getting kind of scratched. Sometimes you don't realize you're feeling restless or depressed until you're faced with the store receipts recording the hideous details of an expensive retail therapy session.

If you find yourself unexpectedly at a cash register or an online checkout page, drop that credit card and ask yourself this: What are you really trying to buy? The answer is rarely a tagine pot or another pair of sunglasses.

Then you must ask yourself, why are you allowing yourself to spend your money frivolously, rather than saving up for a bigger ticket item you really want, such as a vacation or a down payment on your first home? Why would you sacrifice your own long-term goals for such a short-term burst of material gratification? We are certainly not psychologists, but we're willing to go out on a limb and give you a few suggestions to mull over:

- **Boredom.** What, you, bored? How is that possible when your life and your job are so busy? Yet being busy and having too much to do are not necessarily cures for boredom. Whether it's a lack of challenge or too many repetitive tasks, tedium often leads to unhealthy behaviour, such as overindulging in alcohol, cigarettes, chocolate and, for some people, shopping. Retailers are right there waiting with something new and beautiful every time we visit, flooding the brain with that happy-feeling neurotransmitter, dopamine. You need to avoid temptation and channel that excess energy into something more stimulating, speaking of which . . .

- **Lack of stimulation.** There are only so many times you can click on the send/receive button in your email program and still feel a sense of accomplishment. You have learned to sign 20 words in American Sign Language, but so has your one-year-old, which was kind of the point. When you score a great deal, however, especially on online flash sales where you compete against other shoppers to snap up an item before its gone, your adrenalin spikes and you feel triumphant, like you've won a prize. You wait with anticipation for the courier to arrive: it's like getting a present delivered! Uh-oh . . . Find a healthy challenge instead—go for a run, sign up for a yoga class—any means of scoring more endorphins without resorting to your credit card.

- **Depression.** According to the BMO "Psychology of Spending Report," 60 per cent of Canadians admit to shopping as a means of cheering themselves up. If you've ever battled a serious case of depression or anxiety, you already know that you won't master it at the mall. Pay a professional—not a salesperson—to help you sort it out.

- **Anger.** You've seen the way kids misbehave when they are repressing anger. Adults act out their pent-up anger in confusing ways, too. Shopping is one of those behaviours that can be used to funnel difficult emotions into something that doesn't look so bad. Compared to alcohol or drug addictions, shopping may seem to be a minor flaw, unless you're spending money you can't afford, and depriving yourself of things you need. Dig deeper to figure out what's really bothering you—and find a better way to deal with it that's both socially acceptable and won't lead you down the path to bankruptcy.

- **Procrastination.** Everyone has something they drag their heels on: we all avoid the messy, uncomfortable or difficult tasks. Suddenly browsing online for holiday gifts, going out to do the grocery shopping, meeting friends for lunch or heading to the movies have never seemed so compelling. Ultimately, the tough choice is the right one: tackle that awkward task one step at a time. You'll feel so much better for taking the initiative. And in the end, you'll finally be able to relax.

- **Loneliness.** Salespeople may be friendly, but they are not exactly your friends (even if you've Facebooked them). A study out of Taiwan in 2011 showed that elderly people who shopped daily tended to live longer—not because they were shopping—but because they were spending time in the company of others. And while this may have helped with longevity in this one scenario, it's hardly proof that shopping pays for the modern consumer. Indeed, you shouldn't need to buy something (or act like you might) to gain approval. Seek out relationships that are based on *friendship*, not a financial transaction. If you have great friends and relationships, who needs retail?

---

 **THE DARK SIDE OF IMPULSE BUYING**

If all we had to worry about was a little bit of guilt for being greedy, impulse shopping would not be such an issue. However, the BMO report found that 43 per cent of Canadians sometimes spend more in a month than they earn. Our spending habits are getting in the way of taking care of the necessities: 23 per cent said they have been unable to buy something they needed because of their spending on non-essentials. A further 31 per cent even borrowed money or took out a loan to pay for their luxury purchases. And if you think this is all just a matter of income, you're wrong: 19 per cent of those in households earning at least $100,000 a year have been stuck not being able to afford something they needed because of their discretionary spending.

## Resistance Is Not Futile

If you think you can't contribute to your savings because you have enough trouble making your money last to the end of the month, you are probably spending more than you realize on impulse purchases. Here are five tips to help you avoid unnecessary purchases so you can put more money toward your savings:

1. **Never shop without a list.** If you are no longer the analogue type, use your PDA. Type a text message to yourself, listing the items you need to pick up. Focus on going into the store and getting the items on your list, rather than ambling along, aisle after aisle, looking for stuff you *might* need.

2. **Track your cash.** We've said it before; we'll say it again: tracking your expenses really helps you to become aware of how much of your income gets "accidentally" spent on inconsequential purchases.

3. **Shop in reverse.** Once you become aware of those tricky retailer strategies, you can beat them at their own game. Start at the end and work your way backwards through the store. Create an association in your mind between the smell of those barbecue ribs and that MSG-infused, store-bought taste—nowhere near as good as your own home-basted version. Show those marketing dudes that you are on to them.

4. **Resist temptation.** For some people, shopping is an addiction. Alcoholics resist meeting up with friends at bars. Ex-smokers resist having even the tiniest puff, because it could set them back for months or years. If you have a shopping problem, don't put yourself in a place where you'll be tempted. Stay out of the shops and unsubscribe from all those daily deal and flash-sale email alerts.

5. **Do a little reconnaissance.** If you're going out to dinner and have a tendency to overspend on wine, check out the wine list online and decide what to order before you get there. If you need to find a certain item, call around until you find a store that carries it. Not only will your shopping trip be more efficient, but you also will be far less likely to buy extra items that you find along the way.

---

**🔑 GOLDEN RULE: THE CONTROLLED SPLURGE**

Maybe you're feeling restless, you're emotionally drained or you just feel the need to reward yourself for a long period of fiscal restraint. Whatever the reason, you are seriously jonesing for some retail therapy. You've tried everything possible to distract yourself and yet the urge to splurge persists. How to shake this spending feeling? Give yourself a limit—a relatively small sum, such as $20. Get the cash and put it in your pocket. (Credit and debit cards are too dangerous to a person in your condition!)

Now go out and find something to blow that twenty bucks on. Tell yourself you can spend it on anything you want—as long as it's within your pocket cash limit. You may be surprised to find that a stylish pair of socks or stockings lifts your spirits as much as a new pair of shoes. A luxurious hand cream to use every day or a pint of Häagen-Dazs and an hour spent reading the latest *Vanity Fair* magazine can feel as indulgent as an expensive massage at a fancy spa. Turns out there is actually no need to wreak financial havoc merely because of a mood swing.

---

## What's the Payoff?

In case you're wondering, what's the payoff for living a strictly disciplined life? What benefit do you gain by giving up spending everything you earn on fabulous things and abandoning the generally awesome habit of spending your way into debt? According to the BMO report, the average Canadian spends roughly $310 a month on unnecessary items. Respondents felt they could probably save two-thirds of that, or $206 a month, if they simply made an effort to limit impulse spending. That works out to an additional $2,472 a year. Stick to your guns for 25 years, and you'll be able to retire with an extra $61,000 *plus interest.*

### Because, You're Worth It

In 1973, L'Oréal Preference hair colour launched an advertising campaign with the now famous tagline "Because I'm worth it." By 1997, L'Oréal Paris had adopted the slogan for the entire company. Those four words struck a chord among generations of women and have become a rallying cry for self-esteem, confidence and . . . buying power. How often have you contemplated buying not just a hair-colouring kit, but also a pair of boots, a holiday, maybe even a car, and justifying the expenditure with the simple thought "I'm worth it"?

While we have no doubt that you deserve such pleasures in life, this slightly dubious, self-justifying principle can lead you to buy things you can't really afford and put you in a difficult debt position. Even if you can afford the luxuries you believe you are worthy of, tying your self-worth to the accumulation of material goods is a flawed strategy because there will always be people who have more, bigger, fancier stuff than you do. So when you find yourself lusting after some new acquisition and you hear yourself thinking, "But, I'm worth it," remind yourself of the following:

- You are worth having money in the bank and the confidence that comes with that.

- You are worth having an emergency fund and a retirement plan to ensure you won't have to work forever.

- You are worth having a sound, stable and secure financial life.

- You are worth living a life free from the constraints of debt and harassment by creditors.

- You are worth being loved and appreciated by family and friends, even if you do not buy them expensive gifts and instead choose thoughtful gifts within your budget.

- Your children are worth being taught prudent money-management skills.

- You are worth every moment you spend taking care of yourself and your finances. Do it for no one else but yourself.

# 10

## Eat Out

*Treat yourself to dinner out at least a few times a week. It's convenient, it's relaxing and your time is worth something—even if you wouldn't have spent it working.*

Once upon a time, eating out was a special occasion. Going out to a restaurant signalled a special event: a birthday, an engagement, an anniversary. You had to get dressed up and be on your best behaviour. Going to a restaurant as a family was even more rare. Fathers would chastise kids for filling up on bread and value-conscious moms would encourage you to "eat the meat" while noting that the soup was definitely not as good as her own.

Those days are gone. Going out to a restaurant is central to almost all of our social engagements. Meet for wings and watch the game. Grab a quick bite of pasta before the concert. The classic date-night combination of dinner and a movie. For many people, eating out at a great restaurant *is* the entertainment.

Our kids now grow up eating sushi, gourmet burgers and Neapolitan-style pizza. They know their teppanyaki from their pad thai. They think whole chickens always come roasted and ready-to-eat. Edamame beans are the new McDonald's french fries. A few years ago, a *Globe and Mail* article claimed, "We are the restaurant generation."[1] The author cited a credit counsellor who said, "There's no doubt individuals and families are eating out in restaurants about 30 per cent more than they did 20 years ago."

There are many sociological reasons for how we as a society have morphed into the restaurant generation. Certainly our tastes have globalized over the past 20 years. Celebrity chefs such as Nigella Lawson, Anthony Bourdain and Jamie Oliver have opened up our minds to broaden our dining experiences and the way we think about food. But even while we buy their cookbooks and get hooked watching Food Network cooking shows, our growing fascination with food and the food scene inspires us to want to eat out and try new restaurants more than ever before.

In 2012, *New York* magazine ran a story called "When Did Young People Start Spending 25% of Their Paychecks on Pickled Lamb's Tongues?"[2] The story chronicled the advent of "foodie-ism" as an essential part of today's youth culture. The author interviewed a 27-year-old woman who earns $70,000 a year and lives in Brooklyn, where she pays $1,100 a month on rent. The rest of her income is spent on eating out—it's her hobby, her entertainment and her social life. The young woman tracked her food expenditures for just one week and found she had spent $350 at 14 restaurants, pizza joints and cafés.

---

[1] Judith Timson, "As Food Costs Skyrocket, the Restaurant Generation Pays a Hefty Tab," *The Globe and Mail*, March 13, 2009, http://www.theglobeandmail.com/life/as-food-costs-skyrocket-the-restaurant-generation-pays-a-hefty-tab/article672699.

[2] Michael Idov, "When Did Young People Start Spending 25% of Their Paychecks on Pickled Lamb's Tongues?" *New York* magazine, March 25, 2012, http://nymag.com/restaurants/features/foodies-2012-4.

**WHY DO WE SPEND SO MUCH?**

Market-research firm Technomic studied the habits of the generation known as the Millennials (ages 20 to 35), a.k.a. Generation Y, and found that 42 per cent say they visit "upscale casual-dining restaurants" at least once a month.[3] In comparison, 33 per cent of Gen-Xers and 24 per cent of baby boomers make the same claim. When asked why they spend the way they do, Gen-Ys gave answers that perhaps we can all relate to:

- 31 per cent said: "Often I have no choice but to eat meals on the run."

- 28 per cent said: "My daily responsibilities can be overwhelming, forcing me to eat out or pick food up to bring home."

- 23 per cent said: "I prefer picking up quick meals to cooking meals."

## The Canadian Way

Of course, it's not just twentysomethings out there eating up a storm; the trend toward eating out knows no generational boundaries. Nor is it a trend among only the affluent. Those with more disposable income do eat out more often. (Is it for pleasure or because they are so busy earning more money they don't have time to cook?) However, single-parent families juggling time and responsibilities also eat out more often as a matter of convenience.

---

[3] Technomic, "The Generational Consumer Trend Report, 2012," http://www.technomic.com/Reports_and_Newsletters/Consumer_Trend_Reports/dyn_PubLoad.php?pID=58.

Consider this, from a report from Agriculture and Agri-Food Canada:

> *Both total food expenditures and the proportion spent in restaurants increases with household income. Persons with household incomes less than $20,000 spent about 23% of their weekly food dollar in food service in 2001, while those from households with $80,000 or more spent 36% (locally and while travelling). However, there was almost no difference in proportional local and day trip spending by restaurant type (table service, fast food, cafeteria and other) by income group. Single men spent the highest proportion of their food budgets in restaurants in 2001. Lone parent families headed by women also ate out more than the average.*[4]

---

**⊸🔑 GOLDEN RULE: DRIVE PAST THE DRIVE-THRU**

Fast-food drive-thrus are extra tempting when you've got a carload of kids and are shuttling them between school, soccer practice and piano lessons. How to avoid 'em? Keep a list of your standby snacks that you can quickly whip up (a blender full of smoothies in ready-to-go mugs) and healthy items you can throw into a snack bag for the car (granola bars, fruit, cheese and crackers). This will keep the low-sugar meltdowns at bay until you can get home for a proper meal.

---

## Resist with the Help of Rituals

The main reason you reach for the phone at dinnertime or stop for takeout on the way home from work is convenience. You are busy, tired and the question "What's for dinner?" exhausts you.

---

[4] "Canadian Food Trends to 2020—A Long Range Forecast," Agriculture and Agri-Food Canada (website), July 2005, http://stayactiveeathealthy.ca/files/Canadian_Food_Trends_2020_0.pdf. Also: http://www.docstoc.com/docs/56078873/Food-Trends-to-2020.

Enter the weekly dinner rituals. This is a modern twist on classic meal-planning. Instead of planning a rigorous three-point menu for each night of the week, come up with broad categories instead, so you and your family can come to expect, say, pasta every Monday night. The variety of pasta and what you serve with it will vary from week to week, but at least you will have a guideline rather than an entirely blank slate. Your kids will love the sense of control they get from knowing what is coming up as well as the consistency of little family rituals.

Doing one big grocery run a week ensures you have the ingredients on hand for a weekly lineup of easy dinners. For example: Sunday is big roast night; Monday, pasta night; Tuesday, grill night; Wednesday, a fish fry; Thursday is biggie salad night; and Friday is make-your-own pizza night. Saturday is roll-your-own-(insert ingredient here) night. It could be a wrap, sushi, fajita . . . think of the possibilities! Or get the kids to each pick their favourite ingredient and dedicate one night a week to creating a dinner around it.

Make each night's dinner idea flexible enough so it feels more like a ritual and less like a routine. Engage your family in plotting out the weekly categories so that everyone has something to look forward to and can help out. At the end of a workday, having a plan for dinner and the groceries to do it will lift a huge weight off your shoulders and there is a much lower chance that you will break your budget and call the pizza place out of desperation.

## Evaluate the Joy

There is no question that many people derive a great deal of joy and gratification from eating out, whether that means going out for a restaurant meal or merely picking up a coffee and a muffin for breakfast.

Too many financial advisers force you to strip all those little pleasures from your life. You know what we're talking about: the things that make the daily grind smoother and less aggravating. Your daily coffee. Your takeout lunch. Your date-night restaurant meals. Your trips to get ice cream with the kids. Your smoothie from the juice bar after a long run. Your drinks out with friends. Your wine . . . oh, the wine!

If you are staggering under serious debt overload and need to go on an extreme austerity plan—then, yes, you do need to cut out all extraneous costs until you get your budget back into balance. Consider it a classic case of short-term pain for long-term gain. However, if you just need to find more room in your budget, increase your savings and improve your cash flow mojo, then we suggest you do not cut out all of these little expenditures entirely. You need modest pleasures and rewards to make life enjoyable, every bit as much as you need occasional big celebrations.

The solution, as we see it, is to evaluate the joy you get out of each dollar you spend. If you stop at Starbucks every day, it's no longer a treat, it's a habit. According to the economic theory of marginal utility, you don't appreciate a fifth visit to Starbucks in a given week as much as you would enjoy a single weekly indulgence. The same rule applies to dining out. "Ho-hum. Seared tuna with truffled risotto and baby bok choy . . . *again?*"

Now consider this: we are willing to bet you never get joy out of paying bank fees or interest on your credit card balance. So eliminate them. Pay off your balance on time and talk to your bank about switching to a no-fee account. Any category of spending that you pay out of mere convenience, lack of effort or from habit, and from which you derive no joy, is a category you need to review and, if possible, dispose of. This is where true cost-savings come from. Your pleasure in life will be enhanced, not diminished, by eliminating unnecessary expenses.

When it comes to food and entertainment costs, items such as popcorn at the movies, your daily latte, your weekly restaurant meal or takeout pizza . . . these are areas that may actually contribute to your overall happiness. So rather than eliminating them entirely, reduce their frequency to make them even more special, more celebratory and more uplifting. The savings are an extra bonus.

Here are a few examples of ways you can evaluate your joy-versus-spending ratio when it comes to three big areas of everyday expenditure—coffee, lunch and dining out.

## The Coffee Factor

In Chapter 3, we talked about how much your coffee money would be worth if you invested it instead of sipping it. Rather than boldly eliminating all trips to the coffee shop, let's try a more mellow approach. Suppose your average spend at Starbucks or Tim Hortons is $3.25. Not so bad and so much easier than brewing your own, right?

Multiply that by a five-day workweek and you're looking at $65 a month. Okay, but you really *enjoy* that coffee, so maybe it's worth it to you to spend that money on the few stolen moments you take stopping in at the coffee shop and sipping from that steaming cup before plunging into your busy office. But wait, we're not finished yet: on an annual basis, that coffee adds up to $780. Whoa! Who wants to blow $780 on coffee? Just think of what you could use that much money for!

If you love your morning mug or maybe your afternoon coffee break ritual but can't swallow the idea of spending $780 a year on it, try thinking of that premium-priced coffee as what it is—an indulgence. After all, the make-it-yourself variety costs you more like 30-to-50 cents a cup, so in some cases you are paying nearly

10 times the amount for store-bought rather than regular made-at-home coffee. You're paying for the luxury and the experience.

Make it a morning ritual to fill up a travel mug of coffee at home before you head out the door or grin-and-bear the office brew. Save your trip to Starbucks or Tim Hortons for a once-a-week treat. Make it your humpday cappuccino or your TGIF latte. Or, just hold off for those inevitable days when the turkeys get you down and you really need that brief escape to the coffee shop. Your favourite coffee delicacy will taste sweeter than ever.

### Bring-Your-Own Brown Bag (BYOBB)

A survey in 2012 revealed that 61 per cent of Canadians who go out and buy their lunch spend between $7 and $13 each time.[5] A few, 9 per cent, spend $14–25 on their lunch. On a national basis, men spend an average of $9.30 per lunch, while women spend $8.30. Men also tend to head out for lunch more frequently than women. (Note: the survey didn't mention anything about the tendency to go golfing.)

Back in Chapter 3, we looked at the opportunity cost of investing your lunch money. But just like your coffee money, we suggest you might want to take a balanced approach to the way you quite literally spend your lunch hour. With the average cost of a brown-bag lunch around $2–$3, you can see what a difference eating out versus BYOBB can make to your cash flow mojo.

You don't need us to preach. It's a universally known fact that bringing your lunch to work is not only the economical choice, but the healthier choice as well, since your own packed lunch will most likely include fresher food and less fat, sugar and sodium. But

---

[5] Visa Canada Corporation, "Canadians Who Buy Lunch . . ." Press Release, Canada News Wire (website), July 9, 2012, http://www.newswire.ca/en/story/1004763/canadians-who-buy-lunch-spend-8-80-on-average-an-expense-that-adds-up.

just because you know something is a better choice doesn't mean you will make that choice. Here are a few of the excuses people give for not bringing their own lunch:

## Excuse #1

"I pack a nice, wholesome tuna sandwich on multigrain, but then lunchtime rolls around and I don't feel like tuna. I feel like a chicken stir fry." **Solution:** Food cravings are almost always psychologically rooted. Maybe what you're really craving is a chance to get away from your desk. Grab your brown bag and find a place in the park or in the food court where your tuna sandwich will get the appreciation it deserves.

## Excuse #2

"The act of going out and foraging for my lunch gives me a much-needed mental break from the office." **Solution:** If this is the case, then you are relying on choosing between a burrito or a chef's salad as your means of mental relaxation. Really? We think you can do better. How much more relaxing to already have the what-to-eat dilemma solved, so you can truly give your mind a break by reading a book, visiting a friend or catching up on the news over your lunch hour.

## Excuse #3

"I don't have time to think about the extra groceries to buy in advance, let alone the preparation required to pack a decent lunch." **Solution:** Why is it we will do something for our children without hesitation, yet when it comes to providing the same level of care for ourselves, we are too busy to be bothered? Be one of your own kids—nurture yourself accordingly.

*Excuse #4*

"Going out for lunch is important to me from a social perspective. It helps me get to know my colleagues better and sometimes I use lunch as an opportunity to meet with old friends I wouldn't otherwise have the chance to see." **Solution:** The act of leaving the office, slowing down to share a meal and enjoying a casual moment is what provides the social bonding opportunity. The restaurant bill has nothing to do with it. Call it a picnic. Suggest a BYOBB lunch and to meet in a peaceful spot somewhere off the beaten track.

*Excuse #5*

"I like going out for lunch. It's the only thing I look forward to in my day." **Solution:** Uh-oh. If lunch is the highlight of your working day, perhaps it's time to look for a new job! Nevertheless, this excuse takes us back to our point about evaluating the joy. If the money you spend on lunch gives you immense satisfaction and is an important contributing factor to the quality of your life, then so be it. Buy your lunch and cut back in another area in order to compensate. Keep your lunch money under control by setting limits, such as a price ceiling—the most you spend on any given lunch—or a weekly prix fixe.

## Dining Out

If you love dining out and trying all the new restaurants touted in the food scene, it is critically important to keep tabs on your spending. Once you are seated at the table, facing the menu, it's all too easy to throw caution to the wind and justify your overspending as a special treat, only to find yourself overindulging again at a different restaurant a few days later. Not only is this hard on your wallet, it's also hard on your waistline.

*Tip #1*

If it's a special date or a family celebration, consider a long, leisurely weekday brunch or lunch rather than dinner. There is something inherently civilized about an elegant midday meal when you're not watching the clock or needing to get back to work (or to the baby-sitter). At many restaurants, lunch prices are a fraction of those at dinner, sometimes for the same entrees.

*Tip #2*

The exception to Tip #1 is the notoriously overpriced hotel brunch buffet—that $60 per person ($30 for kids under 12!) for an assort-ment of eggs, waffles, sausages and fruit is definitely *not* value for money. Avoid. Choose a local restaurant where even the fanciest brunch dish will not set you back more than $15.

*Tip #3*

Some fantastic restaurant bargains can be found on daily deal web-sites such as Groupon, LivingSocial and SmartBetty. When you're thinking about which of the many new restaurants to visit for your date night, check out what's on offer on the group-buying sites first. A two-for-one deal at the local pub you've been meaning to try might just make your decision for you.

*Tip #4*

Ordering that second glass of wine or a bottle is often the budget breaker. When dining out casually, stick to one glass of wine and make it last. Sharing a half-litre carafe with your dining companion is a cost-effective way to enjoy an extra half-glass each. Never be shy about ordering the house wine or the least expensive wine on the menu. Restaurants take great pride in carefully selecting their wine lists, so even the cheapest bottle will be a respectable choice.

*Tip #5*

Focus on the part of the meal you enjoy most. If you really want to try the crispy noodles at the new upscale Asian restaurant all the foodies on Chowhound are raving about, then go in for an order of noodles and a beer. Who says you need to buy a three-course dinner? If you've heard a certain five-star restaurant makes a killer chocolate soufflé, eat dinner at home and then head there one evening for dessert and a glass of wine. You get all the ambience and pleasure without the heart attack–inducing bill at the end.

## Breaking Bread

Regardless of where you choose to eat—at home or out—sharing a meal with family and friends is a rare chance to put away the cellphones and PDAs and focus on one another. If you're at home, try and make at least one meal a day a family meal, where everyone sits at the same table at the same time and distractions are not permitted. And when you do eat out, whether the restaurant has one star or three is of far less consequence than the person or people with whom you choose to enjoy it.

# Conclusion

## You Earned It?

*That feeling of being on top is something only money can buy. Don't miss out. Money is made to be spent. After all, you earned it . . . right?*

*Reality check.*

*Okay,* wrong! *This is where common sense (finally) kicks in! If there's anything that feels amazing, it's knowing you have money in the bank. The ultimate luxury is not a new car, designer wardrobe or scarlet-soled shoes: it's savings pure and simple. Don't you know that excessive spending went out of style with shoulder pads, teased bangs and "Dynasty"?*

The purpose of eliminating your debt and increasing your savings is not merely to have money. We would never advocate that you live a meagre and impoverished life, only to die with millions in the bank. If you save everything and spend absolutely nothing for your whole life, you will likely achieve a very large bank account. Nothing wrong with that, if your goal is to amass a huge inheritance for your family or for charity.[1] On the other hand, if you spend everything and save nothing, you likely will miss out on achieving your life goals and endure a lot of stress along the way when the cash flow runs dry.

This is why we believe maintaining a healthy balance of both short-term and long-term interests will give you more opportunities to do the things you want to do—now and in your future.

## The Time Is Now

Interest rates in Canada have been at 1 per cent or lower since 2008.[2] Compare this to the average benchmark interest rate between 1990 and 2012 of 6.06 per cent, and you can see that borrowing money has never been so cheap. Consequently, Canadians have been inspired to do exactly that: borrow more money and spend it on cars, holidays and new homes. Heck, load up the credit card and pay it off with the line of credit! Household spending sprees have kept an otherwise slow economy moving.

However, all that borrowing has added up. In October 2012, Canada's household debt reached the same level as those of the United States and Great Britain before their housing bubbles burst and their economies crashed. Around the same time, a survey of Canadians found that more than two-thirds of people polled felt anxious or lost sleep thinking about their finances and another two-thirds admitted to spending beyond their monthly budget.[3]

---

[1] Michael D. Sorkin, "Frugal Man Leaves More Than $1 Million," *St. Louis-Post Dispatch*, June 6, 2012, http://www.stltoday.com/news/local/obituaries/frugal-man-leaves-more-than-million-to-washington-university/article_a43f46e3-85cb-533a-a78d-7e3377d01fd1.html.

[2] "Canada Interest Rate," TradingEconomics.com (website), http://www.tradingeconomics.com/canada/interest-rate.

[3] The Canadian Press, "Feeling Lucky?" *The Globe and Mail*, October 30, 2012, http://www.theglobeandmail.com/globe-investor/personal-finance/household-finances/feeling-lucky-lottery-inheritance-part-of-many-canadians-financial-plan-poll/article4777260.

While the Canadian government and the central bank continually warn us to back off the shopping and get our household debt under control, in reality, only higher interest rates will snap us to attention.

---

**⚷  GOLDEN RULE: MAKING HAY**

How prepared are you for higher interest rates? What will an increase do to your financial situation? When your mortgage comes up for renewal, how much more will your payments cost? Think carefully about piling on new debt knowing that rates can only go up from here. Do what you can now, while interest rates are historically low, to pay down as much outstanding debt as you can before it gets a whole lot more expensive. Make hay while the sun shines!

---

## Cash Flow Contentment

You don't need us to tell you that money doesn't buy happiness, but keeping a positive and steady cash flow can certainly buy you peace of mind. Knowing that you can pay your utility bills and credit card bills every month may not seem hugely interesting when you are 20 and single and happy just to crash on a friend's sofa. As you get older, however, with children of your own, financial stability can mean the difference between a solid night's sleep and eternal insomnia.

Increasing your cash flow mojo, your confidence, self-worth and opportunities is what the previous 10 chapters have been all about. As a way of summing up, we want to leave you with these four principles:

- **Live within your means.** You will never get ahead as long as you spend more than you earn. Find happiness in what you can afford and you are more likely to build wealth that will allow you to increasingly afford more. Teach your children to do the same.

- **Prioritize your resources.** You will never be able to do everything: even if you had the money, you would not have the time. Therefore, do not blindly spend your limited resources. Be aware of the choices you make every time you spend money, and allocate your money to those expenses that contribute to your health, wealth and happiness.

- **Waste not, want not.** Your household is a microcosm of the world. Conserving and respecting your resources means there will be more to go around for a much longer time. Be conscious of how much food, water, electricity and gas you use—and how much you waste. Recycle, reuse and share. Trade, sell or donate what you no longer need.

- **Put your treasure where your heart is.** Be clear about what you truly value and what you want to achieve in life. Make sure your financial decisions and actions are consistent with your goals. Do not allow unnecessary spending temptations to veer you off course. Stay focused on what you want and what you believe.

---

**⚷━ GOLDEN RULE: LIVE AN ENRICHING LIFE**

Make experiences richer by getting more mileage out of what you have. You don't need a full set of matching wine glasses to have a great party. You don't need to give your kid designer jeans to be a great parent. Instead, enrich the lives of your family and friends with small, caring, inexpensive gestures—say, secret notes hidden into coat pockets—that will make them feel appreciated and that they will always remember.

---

## What Greater Wealth...

Managing your personal finances and getting debt issues under control are never easy. The sacrifices you make, the time you invest and the short-term pain you may go through will be absolutely worth it when you find yourself feeling lighter, freer and happier. You will be on a path to living the life of your dreams, rather than feeling the anxiety of never getting ahead. As philosopher and novelist Ayn Rand wrote back in 1957, "What greater wealth is there than to own your life and to spend it on growing?"

We couldn't agree more. It's time for you to own it.

## About Golden Girl Finance

The leader in financial media for women, www.GoldenGirlFinance .com is the modern woman's guide to finance, making the discussion of money and investing real, relevant and relatable—and shockingly entertaining. With a voice that reaches hundreds of thousands of readers daily across digital, print and television platforms, Golden Girl Finance provides the voice of female finance to Yahoo! Canada, Shaw Media, *Chatelaine* magazine and "Breakfast Television." Founded in 2010 by Susan L. Misner and Laura J. McDonald, the goal is to engage, educate and empower women of all ages to take charge of their finances and build lasting wealth.

For more information, see www.GoldenGirlFinance.com

# Also from Golden Girl Finance

*It's Your Money, Honey: A Girl's Guide to Saving, Investing, and Building Wealth at Every Age and Life Stage*, by the founders of www.GoldenGirlFinance.com, Laura J. McDonald and Susan L. Misner, and published by John Wiley & Sons in February 2012, encourages women of all ages to take a greater interest—and play a greater role—in those financial issues that affect their everyday lives and financial futures. Organized by the events that shape our financial and emotional lives—including marriage, raising children, divorce and retirement—*It's Your Money, Honey* is packed with expert information in the no-nonsense style of a girlfriend who's got her financial stars aligned and is happy to share her secrets. Conversational, irreverent and intelligent, this guide to wealth creation, wealth management and financial protection provides the advice that smart women today need to know to take charge of their finances and family legacy.

# About the Authors

### Laura J. McDonald

**Co-Founder, Golden Girl Finance Inc.**

Laura J. McDonald is a communications and brand consultant, as well as the co-founder of www.GoldenGirlFinance.com, a leader in financial media for women.

Laura offers unique insight into how the modern woman consumes media and integrates it into her daily life. She provides the outsider's take on the financial world, allowing her to identify with women looking to take a more proactive role in their personal finances, while at the same time helping the financial community better resonate with this increasingly influential demographic.

A frequent commentator in the press and media, Laura is the co-author of the book *It's Your Money, Honey* (John Wiley & Sons Canada, Ltd., 2012) and financial expert for *Chatelaine* magazine and "Breakfast Television."

### Susan L. Misner

### Co-Founder, Golden Girl Finance Inc.

Susan L. Misner is an experienced financial adviser, as well as co-founder of www .GoldenGirlFinance.com, a leader in financial media for women.

As a frequent commentator in the media, Susan has a unique perspective into women's financial objectives and concerns, which she gleans from her extensive advisory experience, ongoing consulting practice and the multi-generational readership of www. GoldenGirlFinance.com.

Susan is the co-author of the book *It's Your Money, Honey* (John Wiley & Sons Canada, Ltd., 2012) and financial expert for *Chatelaine* magazine and "Breakfast Television."

# Authors' Note and Thank You

We would like to extend a heartfelt thanks to the Golden Girl Finance content team, notably Janine F., Tara S., Chantielle M. and debt expert Stephanie Holmes-Winton, among others. It is because of their expertise, their extensive contributions and the research they undertook for www.GoldenGirlFinance.com that this book came together so seamlessly and with such wit and warmth (we hope!).

And a big thanks (with utmost respect) to our wonderful editor, Karen Milner, and the incredible team that surrounds her at John Wiley & Sons. You are a joy and pleasure to work with. Thank you for your support, belief in and championing of our voice.

# Index